DATE DUE

LOST!

LOST!

James M. Surgener

BROADMAN PRESS
Nashville, Tennesee

Library of Congress Cataloging-in-Publication Data

Surgener, James M., 1931-
    Lost! / James M. Surgener.
    p. cm.
    ISBN 0-8054-5671-6 (pbk.) :
    1. Salvation. 2. Missions. 3. Southern Baptist
Convention—Missions. 4. Baptists—Missions. I. Title.
BT752.S87 1988
266'.6132'001--dc19   87-27140
                                                                   CIP

*To my dear ninety-three-year-old Mother
whose prayer from the time of my birth,
that God would lay His hand upon me
for His world purpose, has been answered*

Foreword

"Jesus? No, I don't know Him." That is the all-too-common response to the question Christians ask of persons they meet in lands around the world.

Even where many may have vague impressions or some general information about Christianity, innumerable multitudes do not yet really understand God's loving purpose for them, revealed and made effective through the life, death, and resurrection of Jesus, and available by grace through faith. They do not know Jesus personally as Savior and Lord.

Bold Mission Thrust is a Southern Baptist endeavor to do everything possible toward making Jesus known to everyone in the whole world by the end of this century. Now, about ten years into the quarter century of Bold Mission Thrust, there are many signs of accelerated missions outreach. But the true and thoroughgoing boldness that will be required still waits for deeper commitment to world evangelization on the part of all Christians.

Bold action in global witness awaits adequate motivation. That in turn depends on deeper spiritual concern and the awareness out of which such concern arises—awareness both of world realities and of the nature and purpose of God.

This book by James M. Surgener is directed precisely toward stimulating the awareness of world need and concern for world missions. His broad, perceptive, and impassioned description of today's world and its spiritual need can jar us awake and enhance the thrust of bold global missions.

Here preachers will find a mine of exciting suggestions for the proclaiming of God's world purpose. But more importantly, these chapters can stir the heart of every Christian to a new level of dedication to God's world purpose.

WINSTON CRAWLEY
Vice-President for Planning (Retired)
Southern Baptist Foreign Mission Board

Acknowledgments

I wish to express my heartfelt gratitude to Dr. Winston Crawley, former vice-president for planning of the Southern Baptist Convention's Foreign Mission Board, now retired, for reading my manuscript, offering helpful information and constructive correction, and for granting me permission to quote from the Southern Baptist Foreign Mission Board Annual Report, *The World in View*, for 1983 and 1984, as well as for writing the Foreword to this book.

Thanks also to Dr. Leland Webb, editor of *The Commission*, for granting me permission to quote extensively from past issues of the magazine; to Dr. Harley Schreck, research associate of MARC (Missions Advanced Research & Communication Center), a ministry of World Vision International, for furnishing me with needed information concerning world missions update; to Dr. Paul B. Smith, pastor of the People's Church, Toronto, Canada, for granting me permission to quote from his father Dr. Oswald J. Smith's books and sermons; to Dr. David M. Howard, general director of World Evangelical Fellowship, for facts and figures relating to many of our world who have not had an adequate opportunity to be faced with the claims of the gospel of Christ; to Teri Busse, administrative assistant of the US Center for World Missions, for permission to quote from Dr. Ralph Winter who is the general director for the center; to Dr. John Allen Moore for granting me permission to quote from his article on

William Carey in *The Commission* of April, 1979 (pp. 20-21); to Betty Barnett, AIF, on behalf of Dr. Harold W. Tribble, for granting me permission to refer to or quote from Dr. Edgar Young Mullins's book, *The Christian Religion in Its Doctrinal Expression:* to Dr. A. Clark Scanlon, director, Research and Planning Office, FMB, SBC, for information and verification of foreign mission statistics updates; to Ms. Johnni Johnson Scofield of the FMB, SBC; Carolyn Weatherford, executive director, Lynn Yarbrough, publications section director, and Betty Merrell of WMU, SBC, for valuable suggestions regarding the promotion of this book; to Dr. Robert L. Hamblin, vice-president, Evangelism, HMB, SBC; editor Ron Johnson, Evangelism, HMB, SBC; Dr. Delos Miles, professor of evangelism, Southeastern Baptist Theological Seminary; Evangelist James A. Ponder, Former Director of Evangelism for Illinois and Florida Baptist State Conventions, and currently president, Jim Ponder Ministries, Inc.; Dr. Wayne North, pastor, Emmanuel Baptist Church, Tucson, Arizona; G. Webster Carroll, missionary to Uganda; Dr. Sherwood Eliot Wirt, editor emeritus, *Decision* magazine for reading and evaluating *LOST!* and finally, but not least, to Dr. Thomas M. McEachin, associate director, Mass Evangelism Department, HMB, SBC; Dr. James E. Talbert, Sr., president, Compassion International Evangelistic Association, Inc. and to my dear wife, Rita, for her helpful suggestions and encouragement in preparing this book. For this book, all the credit, all the praise, and all the glory I give to God.

Contents

Lord, What of Hostage Billions?

Lord, what of the unreached billions lost afar;
What of hostage billions in darkness groping
For the Morning Star;
What of billions held hostage by false instruction,
By misconception, superstition, by false leaders,
By governmental edict, by man against man interloping,
By the cruel tyranny of religious oppression;
What of those many wandering, helpless pleaders,
Billions shut off from salvation's holy blessing:
Men, women, children floundering, blind in the night,
Human beings lost, without the gospel light
Who cry aloud for the Bright and Morning Star;
Shall they forever perish in sin's destruction
Because no one cared enough to hear
Their "Macedonian" call
For someone to them the gospel tidings bear;
Lord, what of the unreached billions lost afar,
Must they perish one and all?
"Son," my Lord seems to answer you and me,
"I My part have done by providing them one Redeemer,
One for all; as One Father-Creator I AM of all mankind;
One Holy Spirit I provide, the Wooing Dove
Who witnesses of My one gospel of redeeming love
Without which no one from sin's bondage can be free.
It is because of sin and rebellion that they are blind;
It is because of their forsaking Me for the false schemer
That they wander in darkest night and cannot see.
But you know that I do not will it so.
This is why My word to them is, Come;
Forsake your heathen idols blind and dumb.
But because they cannot hear My loving call,
This is why My word to you, My children, one and all,
Is, Go:
Go upon your knees to them in prayer;
Go upon your means to tell them that I care;
Go upon your feet to yonder lost soul groping there
When you hear My urgent missionary call."

—JAMES M. SURGENER

From one man he made every nation of men; God "will judge the world (Acts 17:26,31, NIV).

1
As One Man, Multitudes Are Lost!

"Jimmy, as a pastor how can you get your people giving to missions like this?" asked C. T. Edmondson, our director of missions here in Southwest Virginia. He had called my attention to the encouraging fact that the Home Mission Board of our denomination was offering an award of recognition for our church as being near the top ten in our entire denomination in the percentage of increase to home missions giving. Yet, at the same time the church has an even greater increase in its giving to foreign missions.

"C. T.," I answered, "the credit all belongs to the Lord. He motivated the people to give as they did." You see, Christian people act as God moves within them. Just as God stirs Christian messengers to go forth and reach the lost of our world with His gospel of redemption in Christ, in like manner He motivates Christian leaders at home to speak and to work with our fellow Christians. In turn He motivates such concern that will result in their ever-increasing support of those who go out as missionaries. Both those who go and we who support them act as we do because we are vitally motivated from inner conviction.

There is, then, a formula for "missions going" and for "missions support": whether foreign missionaries or spon-

soring home missionaries, we must believe as God motivates us to believe that those without Jesus—especially
those who have never heard of Jesus—are surely lost.

This book is my answer to C. T.'s question. I did go by
a formula—God's formula—as found in His Word. I am
certain that this formula can work only if it is based upon,
and built upon, the basic conviction that every soul on
earth today who is without Jesus is utterly lost. I am fully
convinced, and I teach my hearers again and again, that
all those without Christ are surely perishing in darkness,
confusion, misery, and helplessness, and there is absolutely no other way for them to be saved apart from Jesus
Christ and His saving gospel.

I must agree with prominent missionary leaders that
the basic reason too many professing Christians are not all
out for missions is because they are not fully convinced of
the lostness of all humankind without Jesus as Savior.
Thus, before we as leaders can place before our fellow
Christians what this lostness means, we must convince
them from Scripture about the basic reality itself. To far
too many homeland Christians, the big question still remains:

Are All of Earth's Ignorant Billions Really Lost?

There is, however, no question about it on the part of
Christian missionaries who labor among the ignorant
many. Missionary John R. Cheyne in his book *The Imperative Impulse* needed no convincing. He wrote:

"The task is still unfinished. Individuals, families, com-
munities, whole cultures continue to be born, live and die
without hearing of the love of God and salvation in Jesus
Christ. Most are like a man a missionary met in the Zambesi Valley some years ago. The man was bent low. His
curious eyes had witnessed the ravages of storm and
parched dirt following drought. His face was like an ar-

tist's etching, filled with deep crevices creeping through the stubble of white hairs against his black face. After formal greetings and casual conversation, the missionary asked him, 'Do you know Jesus Christ?'

"The man bowed his head, put his hand to his chin and reflected, 'Jesu, Jesu, Jesu Christo,' he said, 'I think he lives just over the hills in the village over there.' He pointed off to the distant range of mountains. This is all he knew about the man called Jesus. And, of course, a man as old and as wise as he was would surely have heard of him. For multitudes Christ is just a thought of a man on a distant hill, unreal and remote."[1]

Yet, too many Christians who have never been to the mission field and seen for themselves people like this man in the Zambesi Valley say they wonder how we can be so sure that those who have never heard of the Savior are lost. All my life I have heard these who supposedly are Christians who insist, "Surely for those who've never heard of Jesus, God must have some other plan; surely He will not leave them with simply no way out!" It seems to me from what I have heard and read from various people in other localities that this uncertainty is much too widespread and deeply entrenched among professing Christians, even among certain Southern Baptists.

Here's one example: Mervyn L. Norwood, as pastor of the First Baptist Church of Odell, Oregon, told of a young woman overheard expressing her doubts to early comers at Church Training during the week of prayer for foreign missions. "I am not even certain that I believe in missions. Why do we keep talking about sending missionaries?" she questioned. "Why should I have to give my money to send them? Like I say, I'm not sure I think we ought to be trying to change people."[2]

So while past missions accomplishments of Southern Baptists have been noteworthy indeed and are becoming more noteworthy all the time, I feel that we can see much greater gains if more of our people become persuaded of the lostness of all who are without Jesus. Now since many need convincing, and all of us need a deeper conviction, I want us to see unmistakably the scriptural base for the utter lostness of every accountable man, woman, and child on earth who is living in ignorance of the gospel—and chiefly of those held hostage in either forced or neglected ignorance. How can we be so certain they are lost beyond hope if they never hear?

To begin with, Jesus has commissioned us Christians to bear His command to prepare for the judgment to all people. (See Mark 16:15-16; Acts 17:30-31.) We're going to see the biblical explanation as to why all are lost in this and following chapters. Even if the Word of God did not explain the reason for it, Jesus' Great Commission would be enough. Jesus would not command all people to repent or commission us Christians to inform all people of His command, certainly, if all people were not lost and facing judgment. Billy Graham told us students when I was in Southwestern Seminary that we are to evangelize the world not first of all because the world is lost, but first of all because we are sent by our Lord!

But now Jesus' startling message He has commissioned us to bear to every person, "God . . . now commandeth all men everywhere to repent" does have a why and a wherefore. Let us hear God's explanation.

All of Earth's Lost Billions Are as One Lost Man

In his great missionary sermon as recorded in Acts 17, Paul brings out the unity of the whole human race (v. 26) as seen from the historical fact that all humankind sprang from one Creator and from one forefather. The King James Version says, "[God] hath made of one blood all nations of men." Charles B. Williams translated, "From one forefather." Actually, then, the 5 billion[3] souls living on earth today are as one man in their lostness and in their need of the Savior. This is because all originated from one divine source and from one human source. One Almighty God has created every human. No one on earth has evolved independently of the First Cause. Again, God created one historical man initially and all men are descendants of that first man Adam.

Now since Adam fell into sin and rebellion against his God before the birth of any of his children, all we humans, being of one blood, are of one nature with our fallen father. So, necessarily, the nature of all is a fallen nature. This result is because the life is in the blood (Gen. 9:4; Lev. 17:11; Deut. 12:23). The bloodstream transmitted by Adam to our entire human race, his posterity, is a polluted bloodstream. "Wherefore, as by one man sin entered into the world, and death by sin; and so death passed upon all men, for that all have sinned" (Rom. 5:12). Not only are all men born with a sinful nature (Ps. 51:5), but we all sin of our own free accord: ". . . for that all have sinned." Therefore all people are guilty and in need of repentance.

All down to this point Christians hear preached and taught quite often and accept readily enough. But when a preacher or a teacher goes on to affirm that this depravity, this guilt, this lostness, extends even to those who have never once heard of the God of revealed Scripture— much less of His Son—some begin to wonder and others to object. Yet if we accept the general doctrine, how can we deny or even question its particular application to those living in total ignorance of the Scriptures?

Thus Paul preached that God now commands all people everywhere to repent because all people have sinned willfully, voluntarily, and knowingly, so all of earth's billions who are without Christ are as one lost man.

All men know that they are in the wrong. What so many

do not know is that there is one sure Savior from their wrongdoing. Worse yet, the ignorance of many is a forced ignorance.

Earth's Unreached Billions Worship in Either Forced or Neglected Ignorance

Every nation, tribe, and tongue on earth has its brand of religion. Still, those without the gospel worship they know not what or who. They worship, but they worship in ignorance, confusion, frustration, and futility. They worship in darkness, and they worship in vain.

In Athens, Paul found many altars to many gods, but one altar had this inscription: TO THE UNKNOWN GOD. Stirred to his depths, Paul was impelled by God to declare unto the Athenians in their confusion, "So it is about the Being whom you are in ignorance already worshiping that I am telling you" (v. 23, Williams).

If the unreached of Paul's day were worshiping in confused ignorance, how many more unreached are there in our day without Christ and worshiping the same way? How many more are groping for the wall separating between them and God, and groping in thick, unyielding darkness! (See Isa. 59:1-2; especially v. 10.) Christian brother and sister, what are you and I doing about informing the uninformed of the true nature of the God they are trying to worship in their darkness and to no avail?

Come now, if we're going to face reality, how many human souls today are being held hostage, so that they worship in forced or neglected ignorance? Where do they live and by whom or by what are they held hostage from hearing the truth?

As to how many are now being held hostage, MARC (Missions Advanced Research & Communication Center), a ministry of *World Vision International,* states: "There are over 3 billion people in the world who do not know

Jesus Christ as Lord and Savior. Large numbers of these people are not being reached by the gospel because they are hidden among larger populations or because the gospel message has not been expressed in ways that they can understand and respond to.

"They are unreached people."[4]

Dr. Winston Crawley, retired vice-president for planning of the Southern Baptist Foreign Mission Board in a letter to me, referring to our usual concept of a meaningful hearing of the gospel wrote, "I feel sure that more than half of the people of the world have not yet really heard the gospel."[5]

Prominent missiologists estimate there are from 15,000 to 17,000 major unreached people groups.[6] The vast majority have yet to be identified as to just where they live. Determining how they can be reached is the big challenge confronting all true Christians everywhere. The US Center for World Mission with Ralph Winter as director calls for cross-cultural representatives who will take time to penetrate these languages and cultures. "This task"—the planting of churches for the first time among the "hidden" or "unreached" peoples—Winter and his team report, "must be the highest priority for all churches around the world."

Missionaries in Africa, Europe, Asia, Australia, South America, and even in North America, report multitudes who are as yet unreached. Ralph Winter's chart entitled "Unreached Peoples of the World 1985," estimates there are 12 million unreached people in the USA and Canada.[8] Home missionaries in certain of our large US cities report finding people to whom the gospel seems as a foreign language. In my own public-school teaching in various states, I have tested the children and found an astounding percentage of them who had no idea whatever who it was who died on the cross for the sin of the world. In our own United States!

Now who or what is holding these multitudes in lostness?

First, multitudes are lost by the tyranny of fellow human circumscription, since few or no foreign Christian missionaries are permitted in their countries. In Communist and Muslim nation blocs, as well as some other nations, either governmental ban, societal, or communal hostility hinders the people from having missionaries. Such countries are classified by MARC as: (1) closed, (2) partially closed, and (3) restricted countries. Certain countries are closed to foreign mission (but not necessarily to internal mission). Such tolerate neither the sending nor the receiving of foreign missionaries, yet permit up to eight personnel per million to get in without being termed missionaries. Such personnel serve as chaplains or secularly. Certain other countries are partially but not fully closed to foreign missions. In these, foreign personnel permitted exceed eight per million but are limited to under forty per million. Still other countries are not classified as closed or partially closed but as restricted countries. They receive forty personnel or over per million but restrict personnel somewhat to under one hundred per million, and sent-out personnel they restrict to under forty per million.

MARC lists altogether fifty-six countries either closed, partially closed, or restricted as to their receiving of foreign missionaries.[9] *World Christian Encyclopedia* reports 70.2 percent of the world's population as living in countries classified as either closed, partially closed, or restricted.[10]

Yet times, conditions, as well as human attitudes are constantly shifting, changing, and merging into one another. Hard-and-fast rules do not always hold. Until recent years, it was reported that all of the Communist and Muslim nations were tightly locked against foreign evangelization. Recently, however, we have witnessed God opening some of these doors enough to permit certain evangelicals, as Billy Graham and others, to witness and preach behind them. Now evangelical Christians are finding the doors of Mainland China finally ajar, and those returning are discovering that behind the closed doors of human ban God has been mightily at work all the time opening doors of human hearts. Some one million Christians that the expelled missionaries left in China in 1949-50 have now multiplied to an estimated fifty million! With God all things are possible. Our God is both able and willing to open all closed doors, else He would not have commissioned us to evangelize every nation; and He would not have inspired John to write in Revelation 7:9 that in heaven there will be representation "from every nation, tribe, people and language" (NIV). Then certainly God means for us Christians to pray for all closed doors to open to the gospel! "Have faith in God" (Mark 11:22).

Second, multitudes are "held hostage" today by the grim tyrant fear: fear as instilled by the world's non-Christian religions. Billions fear going counter to religious taboo and superstition. Billions fear evil spirits. Billions fear the threat of religious, social, or family ostracism. Billions fear death itself should they embrace Jesus Christ as Savior and Lord. Many held by fear have never heard of Jesus.

Third, billions around the world, including vast numbers in America, are held hostage either by false interpretation or by outright denial of Christianity. This category takes in not only the cults, perverse ideologies, and so forth, but also all distortions, whether traditional or liberal denials, of the true gospel within reputable faiths, Catholic, Jewish, and Protestant. Here the dread captor is deception.

Fourth, all of the foregoing billions combined, plus millions more in the regions beyond of foreign mission fields and millions all about us here in our homeland this moment, are held hostage by the lethal bondage of evil passion, by the awful death of sin, and by the wiles of Satan.

Yet, in the fifth and final analysis, all the multitudes on earth being held hostage today are so held by inexcusable unconcern and criminal neglect. By whose inexcusable unconcern and criminal neglect? By ours, as Christians. Let's face it. Our inexcusable unconcern and criminal neglect to accept the cold, hard fact of their lostness in its full implications is the primary factor that is holding billions hostage at this hour.

But now I hear someone asking, "Won't the ignorance of the billions held hostage dispose God to show them mercy in view of the fact that their ignorance is largely forced ignorance?" The answer is no, not at all, because of certain universal principles clearly enunciated in God's Word. These principles I will mention here and expand in later chapters.

For one thing, Jesus announced a universal principle when He solemnly declared, "Except a man be born again, he cannot see the kingdom of God" (John 3:3). Without the change of heart called regeneration, no sinner can dwell with the holy God. Again, as Peter insisted concerning Jesus shortly after Pentecost, "There is none other name under heaven given among men, whereby we must be saved" (Acts 4:12). These principles are universal and irrevocable, and there are no exceptions.

So in spite of widespread human ignorance of scriptural truth, forced or otherwise, still all unredeemed people are lost, and

Still God Is Now Commanding
All Men to Prepare for the Judgment!

The clarion call of the gospel age is a universal one to repentance. Paul stood on Mars Hill and boldly proclaimed that the times when God in His infinite forbearance overlooked human ignorance were past. He made known to them the resurrected Savior, crying aloud: "Now . . . God . . . commands all men everywhere to repent. For he has fixed a day on which he will judge the whole world in justice by the standard of a man whom he has appointed" (Acts 17:30-31, Phillips).

The crux of Paul's message was that in God's command for universal repentance is evidenced His merciful desire that none face the judgment and perish in guilty ignorance, but God wants everyone to experience that wonderful resurrection of soul and body that God has awaiting them through the knowledge and acceptance of the resurrected Christ. So let us Christians inform our world today.

"Ah, but for those ignorant of all of this to be brought to judgment would mean that God is not just!" I hear some of you who claim to be Jesus' own exclaiming. Would you cover your own responsibility to the unreached by sitting as both judge and jury upon the Almighty? "Shall not the Judge of all the earth do right?" (Gen. 18:25). If you will only dare to turn to the Bible and read with an open mind, you will clearly find God rolling the responsibility back upon you and unavoidably hear Him asking you, "Have I not commissioned you to reach and tell every creature My gospel (Mark 16:15; Matt. 28:19-20; Luke 24:47)? Have I not also promised to be with you, work with you always, empowering you to do it? Have I not proven Myself with all who have already gone out upon My command and upon My promise fulfilling their end of the bargain? Why then have you not yet gone to every creature, bearing My call to repentance and My promise of redemption? Why do you keep blaming Me for what you have not done?"

Recently, God has been laying the burden of this message upon my heart so heavily I have been preaching it in one church after another here in Southwest Virginia. And wherever I preach it, it never fails to arouse considerable discussion of Christians, both with me and with one another after I have left. In like manner, I often hear Christians voicing their determination to do more about reaching the unreached. After I have delivered this preachment, "Those Who Have Never Heard the Gospel Are Lost!" in a given church, I usually have someone come to me and say, "I don't know that I ever heard that preached before, or, at least, not a whole sermon devoted to it." This leads me to raise the question: Is this a doctrine we Christians really believe? If so, is it not, then, a doctrine we are sorely neglecting to preach and to teach, and is this view a reality most basic to a true missions vision? If we who are leaders are sure of this teaching, are we just as sure that all of our people are sure of it? I believe as Frank O. Baugh, pastor of the Exchange Avenue Baptist Church of Oklahoma City emphasized, "There will be no response to the Great Commission from people who do not realize the desperate plight of people who do not know Christ."[11]

On the other hand, when we leaders do faithfully inform our people of this reality, significant increases in missions concern, praying, giving, and going inevitably result. I have seen this proven in our own Wise Baptist Association, especially during the past few years. Our dedicated director of missions, C. T. Edmondson, Jr., along with several concerned pastors and lay leaders, have succeeded well in getting the message of the lostness of humankind across to our people. Such bold challenging has produced some remarkable results. A number of Christians and Christian teams, both youth and older people, have gone out to distant states and distant countries as part-time missionaries. Missions giving association-wide is rising by a steadily increasing percentage.

This brings before us what I believe our churches need most from us leaders: they need to be informed, and they need to be indoctrinated. They need to be informed about how many people of the world are yet without the gospel, and then they need to be indoctrinated to see that until these many are reached with the gospel of Jesus Christ they are lost without hope.

What a responsibility we as leaders have to inform and to indoctrinate our people! It all comes back to us as pastors and other church leaders and, finally, to the one in the pew. Do we actually believe that the billions without Jesus are lost—even those who've never heard? If not, why not? And if so, why aren't we spreading this conviction to our fellow Christians?

One Lord, and his name one (Zech. 14:9); He is Lord of heaven and earth (Acts 17:24).

2
The One God of the Whole Earth

Some four thousand years ago a man with his family departed from Ur in Mesopotamia (modern Iraq), destination unknown. Even so, he pushed ahead stedfastly, determinedly, assuredly, because he had an unstaggering faith in the God who had called him forth to a land that He promised to show him afterward. This man, Abram (later changed to Abraham), left behind his native country, his people, his father's household, and what was likely his erstwhile religion: polytheism. Why? Because he had discovered another god? No. Rather, because One had revealed Himself to him as the God of the whole earth, and had convinced Abraham of His plan and purpose to make of him in his life a blessing to all the families of the earth. Because Abraham believed in the one supreme God over all people, he had a profound conviction of His claim upon his life as well as upon the life of every person in all of history.

We do well to note that sons of this man Abraham have founded Islam, Judaism, and Christianity, three of the world's religions that profess to believe in one living God who is both supreme and personal. But we do well to note more carefully that only one of these—Christianity—is actually true to the only revelation the one God has given of Himself to humankind: the inspired Scriptures. This means that only those of us who, like Abraham, believe God from His Word that our faith like his may be counted for righteousness (Rom. 4:16; Jas. 2:23) are actually saved. All others, however sincere, build their faith upon their own works of merit and upon gods of their own creation, ignoring the one God's sovereign claim upon them.

Yet in spite of their many devout strivings, in spite of their much devout worship in their aggravated confusion, in spite of their pitiful ignorance of God's written revelation—even though well over half are living in total ignorance—not one of earth's billions can ultimately escape the one God's sovereign claim upon them. Because of the very nature of the one God as well as the very nature of every person in His creation, God's sovereign claim must of necessity be, as God's Word declares it to be, both universal and everlasting. Because God is who He is and man is who he is, God's claim upon man, *every man*, is a claim upon his very existence, upon his life as a whole, and upon his immortal soul. It is the claim of sovereign creation, the claim of sovereign providence, and above all, the claim of sovereign grace.

Consequently, the most vital of all life's questions for every person is the question: Shall I acknowledge God's sovereign claim upon me in my earthly life while there is still time to glorify God with my life, or shall I wait to acknowledge it at the judgment when it will be forever too late? Even for the one who has never heard the gospel? you ask. Yes. Even for the one who has never heard.

The One God to Whom Every Person Is Answerable

Zechariah prophesied of the day when all people on earth would openly acknowledge the one Lord and His name, "the only name" (14:9, NIV), when Jesus shall reign as King over all the earth. And when Paul took his stand on Mars Hill, his purpose was to leave the Athenians with no doubt of the one Sovereign of the universe and of His true nature. He aimed to convince them of God's personal relationship to them as their one sovereign Creator, Sustainer, and would-be Savior. He drove home to them God's sovereign claim upon them as seen in His merciful interest in their individual lives in the present as well as in His gracious concern for the ultimate destiny of each.

God's claim upon every person follows from the fact that He is the only God there is. As sons of Abraham, Isaac, and Jacob have long heard, "Hear, O Israel: The Lord our God is one Lord" (Deut. 6:4; Mark 12:29). Paul says in 1 Corinthians 8:6, "There is but one God . . . of whom are all things, and we in him." Then if there is only one God, He is sovereign over all, especially since there can be no god beside Him, and all beings sprang from Him, all including humans. Since He is Lord of heaven and earth (Acts 17:24), certainly He is the one God of the whole earth (Isa. 54:5). Every human on earth, being totally dependent upon Him, is unquestionably answerable to Him and to no other.

In his Athenian sermon Paul continued, "Forasmuch then as we are the offspring of God, we ought not to think" (Acts 17:29) of "the Godhead" ("the divine being," NIV) in terms of human conception. Can the Eternal One, the Infinite One, be projected by human intelligence? If not, then we can only know Him and what He is like by His own revelation of Himself to us. The difference between the God of the Bible and all other gods of all other religions is that "he is" (Heb. 11:6) and has revealed Himself to human beings while other gods are nothing at all except inventions of the human mind or men's deifications of themselves or of others. So whether the projected Brahm, unknowable, impersonal; the projected Allah, almighty, personal; the deified Buddha of old; or the deified

Moon of now, none of them are gods at all. They cannot compete with the one true God; therefore they have no rightful authority over humans, or any rightful claim upon them.

A man in our town said to me a few weeks ago: "The god Allah that those Iranians and others pray to five times a day so religiously—and so sincerely—I have no reason to doubt; he's the same God we Christians worship, isn't he? They've got their one god who is personal and all-powerful, don't they? They just call him by a different name, right? They call him Allah while we call him Jehovah; but he's the same God, now isn't he?"

I answered this man, "By no means. Allah and the true God are not the same. Allah is certainly not the God of revealed Scripture. Allah is the projection of the mind of a mortal man—Muhammad—and of the minds of other mortal men who followed Muhammad.

"Just read the Koran, and study what the Muslims themselves have had to say about Allah." While they do claim that he is supreme and personal, they also portray him as capricious and arbitrary, standing back just waiting for the judgment day, so he can hurl vengeance on people of earth. Even though the Koran repeatedly refers to Allah as "the Beneficent, the Merciful," it also says of him "Allah loveth not the impious and guilty."[1] How different from our God! Avery T. Willis, Jr., tells how difficult it was for his Indonesian secretary who was a Muslim even to begin to grasp our Christian concept of God's love for us and our resulting love for God:

"During our first term of missionary service in Indonesia, we began Baptist work in Bogor, Java, and my secretary was a Moslem. Each Saturday I would read to her the sermon I had composed in Indonesian to see if it was grammatically correct and understandable. Often it was not the language but the concepts that were difficult for her to understand. One day I remarked off-handedly, 'I love God.'

"She responded: 'How do you love God? I don't love God.'

" 'I love God because he first loved me. Why don't you love God?'

" 'I am afraid of him,' she said. 'I'm afraid of him because of my sins.'

" 'I love God because he sent his Son to save me. If I didn't love him, I would not be in Indonesia,' I replied.

" 'But I can't feel love toward him. How can I love him? We have no *penjelmaan*.'

" 'I am so glad you used that word *penjelmaan*,' I answered. 'That is the Indonesian word for incarnation. Oh, . . . now I understand why you can't love God. If God had not become incarnate in Jesus Christ, we could not love him either. But since God first loved us and sent his Son, it is easy to love him in return.' . . .

"After I had talked with my secretary about the incarnation, I told her that Christ died for her.

" 'But he didn't die for me,' she replied; 'he died for Christians.'

" 'No,' I said, 'he died for you. He died for everyone.'

" 'But we do not accept him.'

" 'Nevertheless, he died for you anyway. What a pity that you don't receive him.'

" 'But we didn't want him to die for us,' she said in exasperation.

" 'He still wanted to die for you because he knew that your sins could never be forgiven unless he paid the price for them on the cross. On what basis do you believe you have forgiveness?'

" 'I'm not sure,' she replied. 'We just ask God for it and do good.'

" 'That is good,' I replied, 'but God cannot forgive you

until there is an objective basis for that forgiveness. Someone must die for your sins. The only basis he accepts is the
one that he has provided in Jesus. The Bible says, 'Neither
is there salvation in any other: for there is none other
name under heaven given among men, whereby we must
be saved (Acts 4:12).'

" 'But why did he have to die?'

" 'Because there was no other way for a person to be
saved. If there had been any other way, Jesus would not
have died. The night before the crucifixion he asked the
Father if there were any other way, but there wasn't.
Jesus said, 'I am the way, the truth, and the life: no man
cometh unto the Father, but by me (John 14:6).' "[2]

So Muslims do not accept Jesus as the only begotten Son
of God and the only way to God. To them Jesus is not God
since their Koran in Sura 112 states of Allah: "He is God
alone: God the eternal! He begetteth not and He is not
begotten."[3] Turn to 1 John 2:23. You will find it written,
"Whosoever denieth the Son, the same hath not the Father." Now where does this leave the Muslims?

The Muslim, who is one out of every five persons on the
earth, is just as lost as he can be and will remain so as long
as he denies the one true God and His claim upon him in
favor of a god of his own who is in fact the very opposite
of the God of revealed Scripture. Muslim leaders are
themselves being held hostage by Satan and his Allah
deception, and they're holding their millions of citizens
hostage by decree of the Muslim states.

So then Paul's God of love and His Son of redeeming
love is like no other. Totally self-existing, self-sufficient,
absolute, and unchanging, He is independent of all others.
God who is absolute, God who is perfect in every way,
cannot change and still be God. In order to change He
would have to become other than He is and less than He
is. He is absolute in truth, in holiness, in goodness, in

justice, in wisdom, in power, in love, in everything. As is He who is Father, so is He who is Son. (See John 10:30.)

He is the One who revealed Himself to Abraham as "the Almighty God [*El Shaddai*]" (Gen. 17:1). The name means " 'All-sufficient' . . . as the strengthener and satisfier of His people,"[4] explains Scofield. Ellicott asserts that "there is no doubt that it means 'strong so as to overpower.' "[5] He is the one God, then, who is enough for all who acknowledge Him; and He is the one God who is ultimately overpowering to all who deny or ignore Him.

He is the great "I AM" who revealed Himself to Moses in the burning bush. So is He who is Father of all. Though Paul did not call Him father in this sermon, he implied His fatherhood by referring to all men as "His children" (Acts 17:28, Beck). So is He who is the Son of God. Jesus told His Jewish adversaries, "Before Abraham was, I am" (John 8:58). Paul preached Him as the resurrected Jesus. The great "I AM" is likewise the infinite Spirit whom Paul proclaimed as the One whom neither human temples nor human thoughts can contain.

Here again God is unique because no other god is said to be a Trinity. Neither of the other two religions that are monotheistic and nearest to Christianity, Islam nor Judaism, view God as a Trinity. Muslims do not believe that Allah has a son. Neither do non-Christian Jews believe that the God of Israel has a Son. Not a single faith except Christianity has a God who is a Trinity. Now except for our one God in three persons, what god could be capable of creating the universe and man in it; then what god could be capable of sustaining the universe and man in it; and—most significant of all—what god could be capable of effecting man's salvation from sin?

Southern Baptist theologian Morris Ashcraft, writing in *Mission Unlimited,* explained how the doctrine of the Trinity is most basic for our understanding that all human beings on earth are as one man in their need of salvation by the one God of all people. He summed it up by this comprehensive statement: *"In spite of its mystery, the doctrine of the Trinity stresses not only the unity of God but also the unity of mankind, God's salvation, and human destiny"*[6]

For our salvation, we human beings must have God the Father who sends His Son into the world to redeem man, and who sends His Spirit into the world to regenerate man. We must have God the Son who, being both man and God, is able to die for man's sin and thus exhaust the judgment of God against sin,[7] and who is able to rise from death and reign as man's mediating high priest. Then we must have God the Holy Spirit who alone can convict man of sin, convince him of the Savior, then convert his soul by regeneration.

Then who on earth can logically maintain that any other god of any other religion has any rightful claim upon any man or woman? Does Buddha, for example, have any such claim upon any human being? Buddha was only a man of the sixth century before Christ who never claimed to be God, even though he is worshiped by millions today.

I want all the world to see the God of Scripture as the God alone who is the Most High God acknowledged by heathen Nebuchadnezzar of Babylon (Dan. 4:34). I want all the world to see the one God who is high and lifted up (Isa. 6:1) above all the people (Ps. 99:2), above all nations (Ps. 113:4), above all the earth (Ps. 97:9). I want all the world to see Him who is to be feared above all gods (1 Chron. 16:25), and I want all the world to see His Son as He who has ascended up far above all heavens (Eph. 4:10), and far above all principality and power (Eph. 1:21), and whom He has given a name that is above every name (Phil. 2:9).

Hear Him whose name is Jealous (Ex. 34:14), and who demands of us His creation, "To whom then will ye liken me, or shall I be equal?" (Isa. 40:25), now command humankind, "I am the Lord thy God. . . . Thou shalt have no other gods before me" (Ex. 20:2-3).

He is the first and the last (Isa. 44:6). He, then, who is the incomparable "I AM," who inhabits eternity (Isa. 57: 15), is He who demands of every human on earth, as He demanded of Job, "Where were you when I laid the foundations of the earth?" (Job 38:4, TLB).

He alone is

The One God to Whom Every Man Is Answerable for All He Is, Has, and Does

What man or woman on earth is independent of the one God their Maker? What person living came into the world independently of the one Author and Source of all life? What human came by spontaneous generation, as some like to speculate? What human evolved from lower animal life, as the evolutionists would have it to excuse themselves from God's claim upon them? What human came into being as independently of "the blessed and only Potentate, the King of kings and Lord of lords; Who only hath immortality" (1 Tim. 6:15-16)?

Paul reminded the Athenians that we all are God's offspring. Not only so, but in the august presence of the great "I AM," every person sooner or later must admit, "Without You I am not; without You I never would have been; without You I am nothing."

Further now, what man on earth lives one instant of his life independently of the one God his Provider? If God from any living man for just one split second withdrew His finger from where the heartbeat is said to originate, where would he be? Paul informed us that "he giveth to all life, and breath, and all things," and that "In him we live" (Acts 17:25,28). Then shall any man ignore forever the sovereign Giver or His divine providence? Then shall any man live interminably as though he were not held in life by the Almighty Sustainer? Then shall any man live as though there were no God and never be brought to account? (See Rom. 14:12.)

Yet again, what man alive can order the ultimate affairs of his life? Isn't God the ultimate Determiner? "From one man He made every nation to have the people live all over the earth, setting the times allotted to them and the boundaries they live in" (Acts 17:26, Beck). As to time and times, who can boast, "I have picked my own time," either to be born or to die? Who on earth can change his "time allotted"? Shouldn't every person acknowledge with David, "My times are in thy hand" (Ps. 31:15)? As to location and boundaries, who can brag, "I have determined my own place in life," ignoring that "The Most High assigned nations their lands; he determined where peoples should live" (Deut. 32:8, GNB)?

As Matthew Henry wrote: "If he created all, without doubt he has the disposing of all: and where he gives being, he has an indisputable right to give law. . . . He is the sovereign disposer of all the affairs of the children of men."[8]

Seeing, then, that in God we not only live, but "in him we . . . move . . . " (Acts 17:28) also, what man alive has the right to order his life's affairs without first consulting God? "Go to now, ye that say, To-day or to-morrow. . . . For that ye ought to say, If the Lord will" (Jas. 4:13-15). "For none of us liveth to himself, and no man dieth to himself" (Rom. 14:7). I ask you then, if man determines only temporarily and briefly but God ultimately and finally, shouldn't everyone on earth acknowledge God's sovereign claim upon his life?

But now most important of all, what man alive is not

totally indebted to the one God for his immortal soul? What man or woman alive has God not breathed into their nostrils the breath of life, giving them immortality (Gen. 2:7)? What man alive can escape the reality that he has no existence apart from the hand of Him who made him a living soul? "In whose hand is the soul of every living thing, and the breath of all mankind" (Job 12:10). How often do we sing the words of "He's Got the Whole World in His Hands"?

> He's got the whole *wide* world in His hands . . .
> He's got the wind and the rain in His hands . . .
> He's got the sinner man, in His hands . . .
> He's got the tiny little baby in His hands . . .
> He's got you and me in His hands . . .
> He's got the whole world in His hands.

So I ask you finally, if in God we humanity not only "live, and move," but also "in him we . . . have our being" (Acts 17:28), what man or woman alive has the right to ignore the universal God's sovereign claim upon their immortal souls?

To what end, do you think, has God created every human in the first place? To what end is He holding every human in life? Above all, to what end has He provided for every man His one Savior of the world? Is it not to the end that all people everywhere acknowledge Him as the one God of the whole earth, exclaiming in the attitude of John the Baptist, "There is One 'coming after me' who is 'preferred before me.' He is Jesus Christ, the

One Mightier Than I

"He is One of whom 'I am not worthy.' (See Matt. 3:11; Mark 1:7; Luke 3:16; John 1:27.) Though I've been living my life as though He were not Lord, putting myself and other gods before Him, I now bow the knee to Him and cry repentantly, 'O Lord my God, mine Holy One' " (Hab. 1:12)?

Both Isaiah and Paul join with Zechariah in proclaiming the day when every knee shall bow to Him and every tongue confess Him Lord. (See Isa. 45:22; Zech. 14:9; Phil. 2:9-11.)

But now when do you think is the time that every human being in every land needs to recognize His supremacy? Is it not time already? Is it not time already that every man and woman recognize the one God and His claim upon them before it's too late for them to glorify God with their earthly lives?

Billions held hostage at this hour need to recognize just how great this One is who walks among them unseen, unheard, and unacknowledged. Billions need to recognize Him who said of Himself, "In this place is one greater than the temple" (Matt. 12:6). Millions behind the Iron and Bamboo curtains, millions in Muslim lands, and millions more around the world need to recognize One greater than their Red Square; One greater than their Red Dragon; One greater than their Mecca; One greater than their Taj Mahal; One greater than their Wailing Wall; One greater than their Saint Peter's Basilica; One greater than any place, any image, any man, and any other god: One greater than all else.

Yet how can billions held hostage recognize and glorify the one God and His Son when most of them have never even heard of Him? And how likely are many all about us who have heard of Him to do so until we Christians include them in our compassion and take the gospel to them where they are?

Often the church with declining baptisms year after year calls a new pastor whose eyes are open to the heavenly vision. He begins going out and bringing in many of those from the streets and lanes of the city as our Lord commands all of us Christians to do. (See Luke 14:21.) He even enlists a few others to help him and penetrates the highways and hedges beyond. (See Luke 14:23.) Strangers of all ages, races, classes, and descriptions start pouring into the church services. We can see now where this begins happening in church after church today.

So are the church members overjoyed, and do they all rejoice with the Godhead, the saints, and the holy angels looking down from glory? Most do, but often some do not. Certain deacons and others with them are openly miffed. Even when the church sees more professions of faith, more baptisms, and more influx of new members than ever before in its history, the resentment of the minority continues to fester and swell like an ugly sore. You would think such a worthy pastor would be enstated for life. But too often he is not. Against his own fervent wishes he is often gone. After only a short time and when the church seems on the verge of great spiritual awakening, the new pastor's ministry is aborted by selfish interests.

Why? Why in God's name is God's great work cut short? Because the few refusing to abide by the decision of the majority keep stirring up strife. What they had been saying all along continues:

"We hardly need these dirty-nosed kids here when their parents send but do not bring them." But when parents too begin coming, they say, "These newcomers who are not of our background will water down our doctrine."

In far too many churches across our land, this very same thing is happening these days. But, thank God, sometimes as soon as the new pastor is gone, the majority of the church begins a new church in the same community, and this for the purpose of continuing to reach the unreached. At their first service they see more in attendence than they had been having as a part of the mother church. The one God of the whole earth is still finding those of us through whom He can reach out to the unreached.

The one God of the whole earth has commissioned us Christians to every person everywhere because He has a claim on every person everywhere on earth.

In his profound book *Missions in the Plan of the Ages,* William Owen Carver has this summation of Paul's sermon in Acts 17:

"There can be no question that Paul here puts all men on the same basis before God and affirms most strongly that God is the God of all men, has never deserted any class or race, has not abrogated His claim to any, has not surrendered His control over any, and that the good news of His seeking men in the Saviour is intended for all, as also is the warning of the judgment."[9]

Is the time not here, then, for us Christians to set all people everywhere to enquiring first, "Where is God my Maker?" then, "Where is God my Provider?" and finally, "Where is God my Savior?" Because if we do not, billions held hostage currently soon will be crying aloud, *"Here is God my Judge!"*

I found an altar with this inscription, TO THE UN-KNOWN GOD (Acts 17:23).

3
Untold Masses Guilty Before the One Unknown God

"Is he Chinese? Does he live in Canton?" the two young Chinese girls asked the missionaries. He of whom they were asking was to them the Unknown Jesus. But let me give you Diane G. Woodcock and her own words of this encounter that she had when she served her Lord as missionary journeyman to Macao; she was one of the first missionaries allowed to go into mainland China since the Communist takeover:

My two new missionary friends and I spent several hours one rainy afternoon chatting with two lovely Chinese girls, ages 12 and 13. The stunning realization of a country striving to deny God's existence hit me hard when Bob asked them if they had heard of a man named Jesus.

"Is he Chinese? Does he live in Canton?" they asked with childlike curiosity.

While Bob explained, my heart cried silently, "Yes, he lives in Canton, and he watches over you every day." I held back tears until I was hidden inside my mosquito net that night.

I wanted to buy a raincoat, so the two girls showed us through the streets to the People's Department Store. We should have sensed the potential danger they faced if seen walking with us by the way they stayed a bit ahead of us and did not communicate. But we failed to recognize it.

Inside the store, a woman with a red arm band reprimanded the girls and ordered them out.

They had never heard the name of Jesus before they met us. I prayed they would remember and hide his name in their young hearts until the time arrives to venture out and learn more.[1]

To these two Chinese girls, Jesus and His Father were the Unknown God. Unless washed in Jesus' blood, are they guilty before the Unknown God? What about so many of the one billion people living in mainland China, as well as the more than two billions of other people living in other countries of the world to whom the one God likewise is unknown?

We established in chapter 1 the lostness of all people without Jesus, generally. Let us now examine a scriptural analysis as regarding (1) the state of the guilty ignorance of unreached peoples before God and, (2) the response of God to the unreached in their state of guilty ignorance. In both of these interrelated considerations, our concern will be the question of degree.

Starting, then, with the unreached, we want to explore the question of their degree of guilt, both as proportionate to the amount of light given them and as proportionate to their worsening stages of rebellion against such light. Just what amount of light do those without Scripture sin against?

God's Word leaves them guilty without excuse because

The Unknown God Untold Millions Knowingly Have Forsaken

in favor of gods of their own invention.

To no one on earth is God totally unknown. No unreached person lives in total ignorance. All begin their years of accountability in the plain light of nature. Then just what is their degree of understanding of God, of the law of God, and just what is their degree of discernment between right and wrong as regarding their responsibility before God and His law?

Paul intimated to the Athenians that in their very calling God unknown, even, and in their erecting an altar with an inscription to Him they were admitting their inner conviction of His certain existence. This altar had been "erected, probably, to commemorate some Divine interposition [as an earthquake, for example] which they were unable to ascribe to any known deity."[2] So Paul does not introduce God to them. Rather, he introduces to them God's heretofore unrevealed scriptural name and nature. In so doing, Paul skillfully avoided the fatal error of Socrates, that of introducing to them another nameless god.

Elsewhere, particularly in Romans 1—2, Paul showed how that every human, even one not having revealed Scripture, nevertheless does have a very definite knowledge of God's eternal power and Godhead. (See Rom. 1:20.) God's revelation to the unreached is evidenced by every human's innate sense of Deity and of divine law within and confirmed by every human's awareness that all the universe without testifies of Deity. Both of these the inner person comprehends as irrefutable witnesses to the living God. John Calvin said, "We lay it down as a position not to be controverted, that the human mind, even by natural instinct, possesses some sense of a Deity."[3] Numerous Bible scholars agree that this double witness constitutes not simply a faint glow within but a great internal light, at least before heavy sin and rebellion dim it.

Jamieson, Fausset & Brown's Commentary gives us a good insight into Romans 1:19-20: *"Because that which may be*—rather, 'which is'—*known of God is manifest in them; for God hath showed it unto them*—The sense of this pregnant statement the apostle proceeds to unfold in the next verse. *For the invisible things of him from*—or 'since'—*the creation of the world are clearly seen*—the mind brightly beholding what the eye cannot discern—*being understood by the things that are made*—Thus, the outward creation is not the *parent* but the *interpreter* of our faith in God. That faith has its primary sources within our own breast (v. 19); but it becomes *an intelligible and articulate conviction* only through what we observe around us ('by the things which are made,' v. 20). And thus are the inner and the outer revelation of God the complement of each other, making up between them one universal and immovable conviction *that God is."*[4]

When we consider man's inner revelation coming into contact with the interpretation of God's outer creation, we realize that all the universe, all the world, all nature, as well as providence in nature, humankind, as well as providence in humankind, witness of God to every human being. This God called to humanity's attention after the Flood, "While the earth remaineth, seedtime and harvest, and cold and heat, and summer and winter, and day and night shall not cease" (Gen. 8:22). This Paul called to the Lycaonians' attention, "He left not himself without witness, in that he did good, and gave us rain from heaven and fruitful seasons, filling our hearts with food and gladness" (Acts 14:17).

Joseph Addison wrote of this universal witness in his hymn, "The Spacious Firmament," paraphrasing Psalm 19:

> The spacious firmament on high,
> With all the blue ethereal sky,
> And spangled heav'ns a shining frame,
> Their great Original proclaim:
> Th' unwearied sun, from day to day,
> Does his Creator's power display,
> And publishes to every land
> The work of an almighty hand.

So when Paul referred the Athenians to the "God that made the world and all things therein" (Acts 17:24), he was not striking an unknown chord. Then when he made reference to what certain of their own poets had said, both Aratus and Cleanthes must have come to their minds. Aratus had written:

> With him, with Zeus are filled
> All paths we tread, and all the marts of men:
> Filled, too, the sea, and every creek and bay.
> And all in all things need we help of Zeus,
> For we, too, are his offspring.[5]

Then also Cleanthes had written:

> Thee
> 'Tis meet that mortals call with one accord,
> For we thine offspring are, and we alone
> Of all that live and move upon this earth
> Receive the gift of immitative speech.[6]

Then, when we consider man's inner revelation of the Eternal Omnipotent serving as the interpretation of the divine law written in his psychic nature, we realize that God's creation of humankind—so "fearfully and wonderfully made" (Ps. 139:14)—witnesses of God to every person. Concerning the unreached in this regard (Rom. 2:14-15), Matthew Henry said:

> (1) They had that which directed them what to do by the light of nature. They apprehended a clear and vast difference between good and evil. They *did by nature the things contained in the law.* They had a sense of justice and equity, honour and purity, love and charity. Thus they were a *law unto themselves.* (2) They had that which examined them as to what they had done: *Their conscience also bearing witness.* They had that within them which approved what was well done and which reproached them for what was done amiss. Conscience is a witness,

and first or last will bear witness, testifying of that which is most secret; and their *thought accusing or excusing,* passing a judgment upon the testimony of conscience. Conscience is that candle of the Lord which was not quite put out, no, not in the Gentile world.[7]

In the ten moral prohibitions of Buddhism drawn up by men totally unaquainted with the Law that God gave through Moses, we find the unreached man's own verification of this eternal and universal law divinely written in the heart of every man. Four of the ten are identical with four of the biblical Ten Commandments. They are: "(1) Do not kill; (2) Do not steal; (3) Do not lie; (4) Do not commit adultery." A fifth prohibition: "Do not become intoxicated," while not one of the Ten Commandments, still is a definite prohibition of Scripture.[8]

Upon every human being's inherent discernment between right and wrong, B. H. Carroll elaborated:

> Man, therefore, by the very constitution of his being, has a knowledge of God, law, sin, and penalty. . . . With every man in the world there is an internal sense of right and wrong. Men may differ among themselves as to what particular thing is right or wrong, but all have the sense of right and wrong. They are keenly alive to their rights and keenly sensitive to their wrongs. But there can be no right and wrong without some law to prescribe the right and proscribe the wrong. And there can be no law without a lawmaker. And there can be no law without penal sanctions, otherwise it would be no more than advice. And there can be no penalty without a judgment to declare it and a power to execute it. But every man knows that even and exact justice is not meted out in this world—that many times the innocent suffer and the guilty triumph. Therefore the conclusion comes like a conqueror, that there must be a judgment to come and a wrath to come.[9]

Thus we begin to see how that even without the Bible no one can honestly conclude God to be mere impersonal fate as the Stoics of Paul's day described Him, or mere impersonal force as the John Dewey brand of naturalists of our day portray Him. Neither can anyone even so honestly conclude God to be mere luck or chance as often set forth by both the Epicureans then and the Darwinian evolutionists now. No, even the primitive man, if he is true to the light God has given him, must put the worldly wise to shame.

Even the pure pagan knows instinctively that behind his law, order, and reason within as well as behind the law and order of nature without there must be a controlling force, not only, but One with almighty power; One with infinite intelligence; One with reason and wisdom; One able to will; yes, and One who surely is merciful, the Giver of every good thing, including life itself. Even the pagan must conclude the Unknown Deity to be a living person whom he is like, yet One infinitely greater than himself. Even without scriptural revelation, Dr. Edward John Carnell says, "We know God as that Being over against Whom we are perpetually set, upon Whom we completely depend, and to Whom we are finally responsible."[10]

The double-witness light of the unreached shows them their need of a personal relationship with the Unknown God. His light is sufficient to start them on a search for God. (See Acts 17:27.) Still so, God remains to unknown to some. Jesus the revelation of God remains to unknown to some. Jesus the Way to God remains to unknown to some. And in order to know Jesus they must have the gospel.

But now what does the unreached man do with the light given him? Does he acknowledge God as God? No, he does not. Romans 1:20-21 leaves the unreached guilty "without excuse: Because that, when they knew God, they glorified him not as God, neither were thankful; but became vain in their imaginations, and their foolish heart was darkened." So it is both the degree of the intensity of his light and his unreasonable degree of rebellion against such light that so greviously deepens the unreached man's degree of guilt.

Yet, not only are hostage multitudes guilty without excuse before the Unknown God they knowingly have forsaken, but even worse, they are guilty without excuse because

Lost Multitudes Constantly Dishonor the Unknown God

by their unspeakable perversions.

God's unknown name is dishonored by many by asking in Pharaoh's attitude of contempt, "Who is the Lord, that I should obey his voice?" (See Ex. 5:2.) In like manner, they dethrone God in their hearts continually in order that they may enthrone themselves and their base lifestyles which are a sure index of their perverted thoughts, desires, and ambitions as stemming from perverted hearts. "Professing themselves to be wise, they became fools" (Rom. 1:22).

God's unknown nature billions dishonor by asking: "What is God like?" and then mockingly answering by changing "the glory of the uncorruptible God into an image made like no corruptible man, and to birds, and fourfooted beasts, and creeping things" (v. 23). For this idolatry Paul admonished the Athenians, "Forasmuch then as we are the offspring of God, we ought not to think that the Godhead is like unto gold, or silver, or stone, graven by art and man's device" (Acts 17:29).

Thus, God's unknown nature of truth they exchange for a lie.

God's unknown nature of righteousness, purity, and holiness they dishonor by vile sins against nature. "Their women exchanged the normal practices of sexual intercourse for something which is abnormal and unnatural.

Similarly the men, turning from natural intercourse with women, were swept into lustful passions for one another. Men with men performed these shameful horrors" (Rom. 1:26-27, Phillips).

God's unknown nature of kindness and mercy they dishonor by terrible cruelty one toward another. Nowhere is this cruelty more evident than in their heathen religions.

For example, a missionary told of watching a witch doctor in the Australian Outback confront an aborigine mother and demand the baby in her arms. A woman had just died, and a victim must be found. The missionary saw the mother, her face turned to anguish, surrender her baby to the witch doctor who laid it down upon the hot sand and, in spite of the pitiful screams and shrieks of the mother, actually stuffed its little mouth full of sand until it suffocated.

The religions invented by man are full of fear and dread of evil spirits and of the unknown gods or of the one Unknown God. Heavy sin has dimmed their understanding of Him. Inexcusable perversion has deepened their darkness and bewilderment. Persistent plunging away backward has more and more entangled and enslaved life until "the dark places of the earth are full of the habitations of cruelty" (Ps. 74:20). Cruelest of all are the lies concerning the Unknown God of which Satan convinces the unreached peoples.

So now blinded almost utterly even to the light of nature, the unreached stumble around in ceaseless circles of frustration asking: "Where is God?" His nearness they mock by imagining Him so far away as to be unfindable. In this regard Charles John Ellicott tells us that the adjective in the Athenian inscription means that the Unknown is also the Unknowable. "It is the ultimate confession of man's impotence to solve the problems of the universe. It does not affirm atheism; but it does not know what the

Power is, which yet it feels must be."[12] Still another has interpreted the inscription as meaning in like manner: To the God "whose name is ineffable and whose nature is unsearchable."[12]

Now in the face of such unspeakable heathen mockery and misery

Must Not the Unknown God to Lost Multitudes Make Himself Forever Known?

Why, the very nature of God demands that He respond to both the grief and the guilt of the unreached peoples, and that He respond to the fullest degree. The very nature of God demands that He respond to the guilty unreached either in mercy or wrath, whichever the unreached individual will choose by his or her response.

First, we must look at the degree of God's certain response in saving grace to any repentant person among the unreached peoples. Where there is deep iniquity, there is sure opportunity for amazing grace. Romans 5:20 assures us that where sin abounds, grace does much more abound. "Oh, the mighty gulf that God did span/At Calvary." The degree of God's concern that utterly fallen humans do not have to meet the just judgment of an angry God and eternally perish in their fallen state is seen unmistakably in God's sending His Savior Son all the way from the heights of heaven to the depths of all of earth's dark places, yes, even down to darkest, foulest, and most cruel depths of sin. This Jesus did when He suffered every human's hell upon the cross.

Now God is waiting for the unreached to hear of and to accept His amazing grace. God is a most merciful God. For 120 long years He bore with the rebellion and violence and insolence of the Antediluvians before He sent the worldwide Flood. How long has He borne with sinning nations and with sinning individuals down through history!

How long has He borne with Afghanistan as a nation, and with the Afghans as individuals! In all of their long history, has it ever once been reported that an Afghan accepted Christ inside Afghanistan? The extremely few Afghans who have professed faith in Christ outside and then returned to their homeland have disappeared immediately, never to be seen or heard of again. And now, could this present-day Russian invasion of Afghanistan mean that while God's judgment is fast reaching a climax, still He in His infinite mercy is seeking to awaken the Afghans to their need of Jesus Christ?

This causes us to look, second, at the degree of God's certain response in judgment to any unrepentant individual among the reached or unreached peoples of the world. If God did not reveal His just wrath to the full against sin, where would He be when called to account by judicious little man? When man sins, he knows that he deserves punishment, and when the punishment does not fall immediately, little man invariably cries out in judgment on the Almighty, "Where is God that He does not punish me at once?" The longer God's just wrath is deferred, the more sinful man keeps demanding, "Where is God?" If God never did appear in fullness of judgment upon his sin, would not little man forever exalt himself above God as more righteous than He? "God forbid: yea, let God be true, but every man a liar; as it is written, That thou mightest be justified in thy sayings, and mightest overcome when thou art judged" (Rom. 3:4). "Wherefore should the heathen say, Where is their God?" (Pss. 79:10; 115:2). "The heathen shall know that I am the Lord" (Ezek. 36:23; 39:7).

If a just God must surely judge the sinner in the law, must a just God not also judge the sinner without the law

(Rom. 2:12), particularly since he is not without the law written in his heart (Rom. 2:14-15), and more particularly since he is so persistent in perversely and blasphemously defying both his inner light and the Deity whom he senses must surely stand in judgment upon him? (See Rom. 1:18.) Even though the unrepentant man in gospel lands must be beaten with many stripes, must not the unrepentant man in unreached lands—though he be beaten with few stripes (Luke 12:47-48)—yet surely be beaten with stripes (Prov. 19:29)? And can any of the few or many stripes of a just God rightly be considered light stripes? Oh no, as considering everyone's degree of light and everyone's degree of rebellion against such degrees of light? Romans 2:9 speaks of tribulation and anguish upon every human soul that does evil. What about the cities of Sodom and Gomorrah? Did they have the gospel or any written Scripture? Yet Jude tells us that for their giving themselves over to strange flesh they even now suffer the vengeance of eternal fire (v. 7). Even though, as Jesus informs us, their punishment shall be more tolerable than that of all peoples both cognizant of and rejecting Him (Luke 10:10-14 *ff.*), the judgment of God upon all rebellion against plain light—whether the plain light of Scripture or the plain light of nature—is both certain and awful.

But have you never wondered why that God has not already revealed Himself in wrath upon the many, including the unreached peoples, who keep mocking His justice by adding sin to sin, perversion to perversion, cruelty to cruelty, blasphemy to blasphemy? The answer is because God would much prefer to reveal Himself in mercy.

If a just God is now fast responding to the full degree of wrath toward the unreached peoples who remain unrepentant, is not a mercifully just God not likewise now fast responding to the full degree of saving grace toward the unreached peoples who upon hearing the gospel are now calling upon His name in saving faith?

But what of billions held hostage who have never yet heard? How shall they call upon Him of whom they have not heard? (Consider Rom. 10:13-15.) Is their guilty ignorance of the one Unknown God not indeed grevious? Still another suggested interpretation of the Athenian inscription has been: *"To the God whom it is our unhappiness not to know."*[13]

I, even I, am the Lord; and beside me there is no saviour (Isa. 43:11). [Paul] preached unto them Jesus and the resurrection (Acts 17:18).

4
The One Savior of the World

"I'm thinking about founding a new religion of my own of which I'm to be the savior," a skeptic one day said facetiously to a Christian, trying to feel him out with teasing mockery. "After all, one religion is as good as another, and one savior is as good as another. Right?"

"Wrong," replied the Christian.

"Oh, come on now. What do you propose that I do to get started?"

"Well, it seems to me that if you're really serious about becoming the savior of your new religion, you are already off to a poor start."

"How so?"

"Well now, have you been conceived of God's Holy Spirit and born of a virgin?"

"No; but now wait a minute . . . !"

"Then you are off to a bad start. Because if you're not both God and man at the same time, I think you'll soon find yourself meeting some pretty tough challenges. You may find it rather difficult to heal all manner of human ills and even more difficult to raise people from the dead."

The skeptic regarded the Christian narrowly and began to grin, but only because he could find no words for an answer. Finally, he said, "OK, since in your words I'm off to a bad start, what do you suggest I do to remedy my situation?"

"Your biggest challenge, you're going to find, is still ahead of you. If you actually intend to have any significant power in your new religion, you're going to have to have saving power in your name. And in order to get saving power in your name it is imperative that you get yourself nailed to a cross and die for the sin of the world."

To save face, the skeptic threw back his head and laughed loudly. Then while he was searching for an answer to this, the Christian added: "So now, if you and your new religion are to have any possible authority, then, after you have died for the sin of the world, you must by all necessity rise from the dead on the third day."

The skeptic stood wagging his head in disbelief. At last he conceded, "That's a mighty tall order!"

"You can believe it is," emphasized the Christian. "This is why that only one Savior in all the universe fits the bill. His name is Jesus Christ. In Isaiah 43:11 He declares, 'I, even I, am the Lord; and beside me there is no saviour.'"

In Athens and everywhere else he went, Paul preached Jesus as the one Savior of all men, and Jesus' resurrection as the one irrefutable proof of His unique saviorhood, proclaiming, "For other foundation can no man lay" (1 Cor. 3:11). Then in Ephesians 3:17-19, Paul gave as the reason for Jesus' voluntary saviorhood the four-dimensional love of God. Each of these four dimensions Jesus explained to Nicodemus in John 3:13-16. He began with the incredible downward dimension: "He that came down from heaven, even the Son of man" (v. 13).

I challenge any man of any world religion to answer now,

What Other Savior Ever
Came Down from Heaven to Earth?

What god ever conceived by human ingenuity has ever cared enough even to look down with pity upon man guilty and groveling in his desperate predicament, much more to stoop down to help, or—of all things—actually to come down from the skies to redeem him? Do you see Allah doing so? Then, too, what mere man among the many would-be messiahs running around today has ever ascended into heaven, and afterward come down again with divine credentials as a savior of his fellowmen? Do you think Sun Myung Moon has? Jesus forever eliminated the possibility, declaring, "No man hath ascended up to heaven, but he that came down from heaven" (John 3:13).

No wonder that when Jesus came down as God incarnate in human flesh the angel had to announce "Behold, I bring you good tidings of great joy, which shall be to all people. For unto you is born this day in the city of David a Saviour, which is Christ the Lord" (Luke 2:10-11). The Lord's angel had informed Joseph, "Thou shalt call his name JESUS for he shall save his people from their sins" (Matt. 1:21). Jesus' very name means "Savior." His divine title *Christ* means "the anointed One." He is the only one living anointed of His Father God to be the Savior of the world.

Jesus is Shiloh of whom Jacob prophesied (Gen. 49:10). One interpretation of Shiloh is "God-sent." The apostle John wrote, "We have seen and do testify that the Father sent the Son to be the Saviour of the world" (1 John 4:14). What other god so loved the world?

Not only was Jesus God-sent, but He Himself came of His own choosing. In Isaiah 43 God sets forth Jesus' messianic mission as threefold: (1) to declare, (2) to save, and (3) to show (vv. 11-12).

Exactly what did Jesus come down to declare to man? He came down to declare the eternal counsel of the Godhead, that He Himself is the Savior "Lamb slain from the foundation of the world" (Rev. 13:8).

Jesus' self-emptying descent (Phil. 2:5-8) whereby He retained His divine attributes under human limitations forever sets Jesus apart as the one Savior of the world. But just how far down must He descend in order to fully declare the eternal counsel of His saviorhood? My dear old Carson-Newman professor Russell Bradley Jones told us in his book *Gold from Golgotha:* "The inspired writers assure us that this Saviour started His journey in search of the lost, from heaven's throne itself! And He did not reach your need and mine until He got to the place of Godforsakeness! Only there, in the outer darkness of God's neglectfulness, did the Celestial Traveler reach Journey's End! All the while, He knew that to be His destination. He deliberately started out for that point. He was not taken by surprise, nor did He turn from a straight path leading from the throne to the pit."[1]

Now in order for Jesus to descend into the awful depths to save lost humanity it was necessary that He be lifted up to die upon a cross. Thus, I again challenge any person to answer,

What Other Savior Ever Was Lifted Up to Die in the Sinner's Place?

We now have come to the marvelous upward dimension of God's love that Jesus went on to describe to Nicodemus so vividly in John 3:14, "As Moses lifted up the serpent in the wilderness, even so must the Son of man be lifted up." Jesus was explaining to Nicodemus that as surely as those Israelites—bitten of deadly snakes and nearing physical death in the wilderness—required a remedy, just as surely the entire human race—bitten of the fatal

venom of sin and both spiritually dead already and nearing the second and final spiritual death—requires a savior.

Man is facing final death as the penalty of his sin. His
fever rising and the cold sweat already upon his brow, he
is fast plunging to the fathomless depths. But just as surely
as God provided a remedy for those dying Israelites in
Moses' day, He is providing a remedy for all mankind
today. His remedy is Jesus the Crucified One, the One
lifted up to die in the place of guilty man. And just as
surely as Moses' snake of brass identified both with the
sinful Israelites and with their deathly malady, just so
Jesus by His being lifted up to die in man's stead identifies
Himself both with sinful man and with the deadly sin of
man. Lifted up "in the likeness of sinful flesh" (Rom. 8:3),
He "who knew no sin" (2 Cor. 5:21) is made to be sin for
us.

Spurgeon explained that though Christ was not guilty,
He was not only treated as a sinner, but He was treated
as if He had been sin itself in the abstract. "Who would
know God's hate of sin must see the Only Begotten bleeding in body and bleeding in soul even unto death . . . . 'He
hath made him to be sin for us.' Oh, depth of terror, and
yet height of love!"[2]

Jesus was lifted up in His obedience to His Father even
unto death that He might lift fallen humanity up from the
foulest depths of depravity to the most blessed heights of
glory with our Lord Jesus in His exaltation (Phil. 2:8-9).
"And I, if I be lifted up from the earth, will draw all men
unto me" (John 12:32). Oh, the magnetic lifting power of
the uplifted Christ! Oh, the upward dimension of God's
love!

By His tasting death for every person, Jesus is able to
uplift anyone who will look up to Him in saving faith
today, even as He did those Israelites who looked up to
Moses' snake of brass in saving faith.

But now what other messiah whom people worship was ever thus uplifted to taste death for every other person? Was Lenin? No. Lenin died of three successive strokes.

Then, further, I challenge any human being to answer,

What Other Savior Extends His Arms to All Men of All Nations?

Oh, but Jesus does! See Him there on the cross before all people uplifted. His arms extend on the crossbeams to all mankind in the globe-girdling breadth dimension of God's redemptive love. Listen! Hear Him inviting all people to Him: "Look unto me, and be ye saved, all the ends of the earth: for I am God, and there is none else" (Isa. 45:22).

This is the assurance that Jesus gave to Nicodemus in John 3:16, as to the amazing outward reach of God's love: "For God so loved the world." Jesus is Shiloh to whom the gathering of all believing peoples of all nations is. Not only Nicodemus has He invited to Him, but always—before, during, and ever since His crucifixion—Jesus has been extending His arms to every individual of every nation and kindred and people and tongue.

Always during His earthly ministry Jesus included all nations, not just the Jews, in His boundless compassion. The first people to acknowledge Him as the Savior of all people were not the Jews but the despised Samaritans. After Jesus had offered Himself as the Living Water to the Samaritan woman of Sychar, and she, upon accepting Him had gone forth as the first missionary to tell others than Jews of His coming, the Samaritan men flooded the hillsides, flocking to Jesus. As soon as they had seen and heard Him, these men exclaimed, "Now we believe . . . for we have heard him ourselves, and know that this is indeed the Christ, the Saviour of the world" (John 4:42).

See the one Liberator of human souls extending His

arms to billions held hostage around the world today. Look to Him. He alone can unlock closed doors. He alone can break the bonds of sin. He alone can set the captives free.

But how can Jesus extend His arms to everyone everywhere today except as we Christians extend our arms to all? One way to extend our arms to those we are not reaching is by beginning a church bus ministry. You will usually find those among your members lacking faith who will contend loudly and stubbornly that "it just won't work for our church." But even if your church is a small rural church as my home church of Silver Leaf is, God can make it work if we will only obey and trust Him.

A number of their pastors and members kept urging Silver Leaf to step out on faith and put God to the test. But here in this Southern Baptist church of long standing situated high on a hill among the hills of Lee County, Southwest Virginia, most of the members hesitated in unbelief. Then the church called young Ronnie Owens as pastor. Somehow God's Holy Spirit used Ronnie to lead the people to take the step of faith. Soon the church had purchased and was operating a big school bus. A little later, they added two smaller vans. By faith and works the church permitted their Lord Jesus to use those three buses to extend His arm through the people's arms throughout much of that farming community and into those hills and hollows between the hills. Church attendance began to swell beyond everyone's expectation as lost soul after lost soul reached out to take the Savior's extended arms.

It won't work for a little country church? Just ask the members of Silver Leaf.

See the one Great Physician reaching out His hands to you, sin-sick humanity. Hear the one Light of the world offering you sight, blind humanity. Behold the one Bread of life willing to satisfy you forever, starving world.

In his book *What a Savior!* W. A. Criswell observed: "The cross is the incomparable invitation of God to the people of the whole world, for the arms of the cross are extended on either side, wide as the world is wide. . . .

"The arms of the cross reach out for us all."[3]

Now, above all, I challenge any individual of any world religion to answer me,

What Other Savior Reigns Today with a Resurrection Claim on All Mankind?

What other god or what other messiah has ever made it back from the grave? Oh, but Jesus has!

From all eternity Jesus determined to make it back. This is why He could assure Nicodemus, even before His crucifixion, of the wondrous ever-onward dimension of God's love. This is why He could offer Nicodemus His "everlasting life" in John 3:16. Only He who lives from all eternity to all eternity could thus know and speak of God's eternal love: His own love. Jesus' death is the assurance of God's eternal love. Jesus' resurrection is the final proof that He has all authority to give to "whosoever believeth in him . . . everlasting life." His everlasting life is the gift of His everlasting love.

Yet neither His life nor His love could be everlasting if He had not made it back from the grave, victorious over all of His and humanity's most powerful foes: sin, death, hell, and Satan. But Jesus did make it back! Once and for all He emerged the Victor.

This is why Jesus reigns today at the Father's right hand, awaiting His Father's promise to give Him the heathen for His inheritance and the uttermost parts of the earth for His possession (Ps. 2:8).

Not only does Jesus claim all mankind by right of His

sovereign creation, His sovereign providence, and His sovereign grace, but His resurrection claim is His weightiest claim of all. This is because when Jesus rose up from the dead to live forever in the ever-onward dimension of God's love, everyone in all the world in all of history, having died potentially with Him in His death, rose up potentially with Jesus in His resurrection. (See 2 Cor. 5:14-15.)

What other savior reigns today with such resurrection right to claim all mankind for himself?

I once heard an airplane pilot tell of seeing a rainbow as it really is. While flying from the correct vantage point above the earth he saw God's rainbow for the first time as a complete circle. He related what a spectacle of magnificence it was to behold. So it is that if any person will see God's four-dimensional redemptive love of which Paul wrote in Ephesians 3, he must view it from the correct perspective. He must view it from the cross. Even so, he cannot see the love of God in full since each dimension thereof is infinite. But if anyone will kneel at Calvary, he can see each of the four dimensions clearly, and he can see where they meet and cross. He can see the four dimensions emanating from a Person. And he can see the point in time where this central Person of history made God's great love available to all mankind. Dear lost world, just how great is God's love? Look at Jesus dying on Calvary. There He declares. There He saves. There He shows.

Barring the path of any person daring to suggest, "For those who have never heard the gospel God must surely have some other way," stands the Crucified One with His unequivocal pronouncement: "I, even I, am the Lord; and beside me there is no saviour" (Isa. 43:11).

So that they might search for God, possibly they might grope for Him, and find Him (Acts 17:27, Williams).

5
The Lost Groping for the One Savior

Williams has in our text the word *possibly:* "They ... search for God, possibly they might ... find Him" Most translations have it "perhaps" they might find Him. Phillips puts it, "In the hope that. . . ." Here we have before us the age-old question raised by Zophar in the Book of Job, "Canst thou by searching find out God?" (11:7).

Certainly, the Bible teaches that no one can search God out to full understanding. But by one's own unaided effort can anyone search God out to a personal encounter? What about the individual without the gospel? Has any one of the outstanding thinkers, philosophers, or religious seekers of all of history found out God by his own unaided effort? By his own reasoning, by his own ingenuity, by his own religious striving can a man find God? Definitely not.

Why not? Is it because God is so far from humanity? In our fuller text Paul went on to assert that God is not far from anyone. Yes, but the lost man is very far from God! The distance between lost persons and God is far greater than anyone realizes. The breach is far wider and far more serious than anyone reckons. Between the lost person and God yawns the dread chasm of sin. No one by himself has ever spanned that awful gap, and by himself no man ever will.

Not only has sin separated human beings from God, but the alienation of sin has so blinded man's spiritual understanding that his searching for God is that of groping in heavy darkness. Now if the darkness in which even the lost in gospel lands grope is heavy, how much heavier is the darkness in which those in lands without the gospel grope?

Well then, if lost man can never find God on his own as groping in such intense darkness, why—as Paul preached in Athens—does God so encourage man to grope for Him, to seek to find Him?

Why, for one reason,

The Lost Groping for the Desire of All Nations

intensifies their desire. Before a person can ever be saved he first must strongly desire Someone to save him. Do you think that you ever would have met Jesus if first you had not strongly desired Jesus? All of God's goodness to people ought to arouse in them a desire for God" that they might search for God," that "they might grope for Him" (Acts 17:27, Williams).

Haggai prophesied of the coming of One able to fulfill the desire of every person of every nation. He called Him "the desire of all nations" (2:7). The need, the desire of every soul, Jesus alone can satisfy.

This is why, as they watched the hordes of humanity falling over one another to touch even the hem of Jesus' robe, the jealous Pharisees complained, "Behold, the world is gone after him" (John 12:19). So it has been with people of every culture, every strata of society, every race, every clan of every nation ever since. As soon as they first hear of a Man named Jesus they begin overrunning the landscape and flooding the highways. They must see Him, or, at least, they must hear an ambassador of His proclaiming Him. So it is with men, women, boys, and girls of every nationality to this day. "Sir, we would see Jesus" (John 12:21) is not the desire of the Greeks alone. The report that the disciples brought to Jesus was, "All men seek for thee" (Mark 1:37).

Very likely Haggai referred not only to Jesus' first coming but to His second coming as well. He may very well have made reference also to Jesus' coming into the life of every individual willing to receive Him.

Before Jesus would come, Haggai wrote, there must necessarily come a great shaking. Heaven and earth must be shaken. The nations must be shaken. Man himself must be shaken as he observes the nations shaken by internal and international judgments, and most of all as he observes heaven and earth shaken by the voice of God. Before Jesus' coming, man's heart and attitude must undergo thorough preparation. Events in his life must reveal to him what he needs and desires above all else. So it was when God prepared the world for Jesus' first coming. So it is as He is preparing the world for Jesus' second coming. So it is as God prepares an individual for Jesus' coming to Him as His Lord and Savior. Men need to desire the Desire of all nations that they might seek Him, and they need to seek Him that they might desire Him the more.

For another reason,

The Lost Feeling Around for the Rose of Sharon and the Lily of the Valley

awakens their conscience. By creating in every individual a conscience (the spirit of discernment between right and wrong, called in Proverbs 20:27, "the candle of the Lord"), God has arranged that man might detest his own sinfulness and his own inadequacy. As stirred up by his conscience, the unreached man craves and feels around for his unknown Lord as his righteous Opposite and his perfect Counterpart. *The Good News Bible* tells us why

God Himself fixed beforehand the exact times and the limits of the places where all races of mankind would live. "He did this so that they would look for him, and perhaps find him as they felt around for him" (Acts 17:27).

Years of groping about and feeling around have developed in lost billions a keen sensitivity to their utter sinfulness and their absolute need of a savior. Their burden of guilt bearing them down, they turn to their own "holy men."

Speaking at the Pastors' Conference of the 1978 Southern Baptist Convention, our Foreign Mission Board's Joe Underwood told of seeing a man one day sitting on a stool before a heathen shrine. The man was there seeking propitiation for his sin. Brother Underwood watched as "holy men" fastened needles all through the man's chest, back, abdomen, arms, and legs. Then he saw them drive a long, silver needle from one of his cheeks to the other. The man protruded his tongue so that another needle could be shot behind his tongue to hold it that way. Finally, the "holy men" set a heavy steel cage down over the man's shoulders. When the man then got up and walked from one holy place to another, sharp spikes in the cage pierced his stomach with every movement he made. Yet, as sensitive as the man evidently was to his guilt and need of a savior, to Brother Underwood he did not seem even remotely aware of *the one true Savior.*

Every lost man feels an inner compulsion to feel around in his spiritual darkness for Someone who is altogether what he himself is not. Though billions have never heard of Him, that Someone in a Book billions have never read calls Himself "the rose of Sharon, and the lily of the valleys." Even though in Solomon's Song (2:1), the church (the bride) is speaking, how can the church be a rose or a lily except in imitation of and in likeness to her great Counterpart? Therefore above all others the Rose and the

Lily is Jesus Christ. As above all other plants, the rose and the lily stand unique, above all created beings Jesus Christ stands unique. That aching need which lost souls the world over feel deep inside can only be supplied by Him who says, "I am the rose of Sharon, and the lily of the valleys."

Hostage billions living in the filth and ugliness of sin and in the deprivation that results from sin crave above all else forgiveness, purity, and beauty. If they could know their own hearts, they would realize that their deep heart longings can be satisfied only by One who is the personification of goodness and beauty. Of Him alone can it be said, "How great is his goodness, and how great is his beauty!" (Zech. 9:17).

Then for a further reason, God encourages lost people to grope for Him because He knows that

The Lost Reaching Out for the Shadow of the Great Rock in a Weary Land

can have revealed to them a sense of how futile their lives are without Him. Not only inner need, but outer realities as well, ought to turn lost persons in a sense of desperation to seek salvation in their Maker. Every dread hurricane, tornado, and tidal wave of nature, as well as every dread tyranny, oppression, and enslavement of his fellowman ought to drive lost man to seek refuge in Him who is man's one hiding place. Again, every deadly desert of earth, as well as every deadly depredation of his fellowman, ought to turn lost man to Him whose Spirit is as rivers of water in a dry place. Then, too, every volcanic eruption, every famine, every burning drought, as well as every human greed, theft, and atrocity, ought to reveal to lost man his desperate need to seek relief in the shadow of Him who is as a great rock in a weary land. (See Isa. 32:2.)

If everyone is overwhelmed by the fear of the acts of

nature and of their fellow humans, how much more is the lost person—and even yet more the lost, unreached person—overwhelmed?

God in His infinite wisdom knows that never will anyone—enlightened or unenlightened—reach out for the shadow of the Almighty until awesome realities, without as well as within, cause him to tremble in the realization of his own extremity. Why did God foreordain every man's time and place? The *New International Version* answers in our text: "God did this so that men would seek him and perhaps reach out for him and find him" (Acts 17:27).

Yet, for the utmost reason, God encourages lost people in their darkness to reach for Him because He knows that

The Lost Looking for the Friend
Who Sticks Closer Than a Brother

have revealed to them their utter hopelessness without the helping kindness from One beyond themselves. God knows that for everyone there comes a day when the bottom falls out of life. Now if for the Christian this day is called "the evil day" (Eph. 6:13), what should this day be called for the lost person who, unlike the Christian, has no divine friend to whom he can turn? Then what do you suppose this day should be called for the lost, unreached person who must wonder if any Divinity exists who is his friend?

What do you imagine takes place in the thinking of the unreached one when death claims a close friend or loved one? A father dies, or a mother dies; or a child or a husband or a wife dies. What then? What a vast difference there is between Christians and the unreached at such an hour! Paul assured Christians that we have no need to be "as others which have no hope" (1 Thess. 4:13). We have faith; we have "that blessed hope" (Titus 2:13); we have blessed assurance. Above all, Christians have the "friend that sticketh closer than a brother" (Prov. 18:24).

But when the unreached faces the hour of death, either the death of someone dear to him, or his own death, what does he have to cling to? To whom can he turn? Do you suppose he never cries out from deep inside, "Oh, that I had a God that I could turn to as a friend who would become real to me; oh, that I might fall at His feet; oh, that He might assure me of His everlasting acceptance"?

Why has God planted a longing for such a friend in the breast of everyone in history's every stage and in earth's every locale? *The Holy Bible in the Language of Today* answers in our text, "That they should look for God and perhaps feel their way to Him and find Him" (Acts 17:27 *a*, Beck).

And yet how can they find their divine friend without a missionary?

My first cousin G. Webster Carroll, who is a Southern Baptist missionary to Uganda, tells of a heart-rending experience he had while serving as one of God's first missionaries to Tanzania (then Tanganyika). One day an African man approached Webster and his fellow missionaries with a disheveled appearance and in an obvious state of weariness. Evidently he had traveled a long distance. Upon questioning the man, Web learned that he had walked a hundred miles. The man told him he was there as a representative of his remote jungle tribe. He had come to beg the Christian missionaries for one of them to become a messenger to his tribe. "We have heard that you proclaim the Savior of men's souls," he reported. "Our tribe yearns to hear of this one Savior too. For a long time we have waited in the hope that some spokesman of His would come and tell us of Him."

The few missionaries in Tanganyika looked at the man aghast. They knew they were fully occupied with reaching the many tribes all around them, near at hand. Web felt his heart heavy. What was he going to tell this man? Finally, he found words to begin. "You and your tribe must wait for now." Wincing at the disappointment written all over the man's face in capitol letters, Web tried to explain: "Until more Christians in our homeland volunteer as foreign missionaries and until more Christians in our homeland provide more prayer and more financial support for those of us who volunteer to come as missionaries, we have no way we can help you and your tribe!"

How would you have felt if you had been in Web's place and had been the one to convey this sad report of your fellow Christians back in America?

I was happy to read in the April, 1980, issue of *The Commission* that as of June of 1979 Project Sukuma of Southern Baptist Foreign Missions began reaching more of the remote tribes in Tanzania. I do not know if the tribe of the man who came to Webster Carroll has yet been reached, but I do know there are many more tribes yet to be reached. Joy Neal reported that in a short period of time almost 3,000 persons trusted Christ. "In a population of 4.5 million, however, 3,000 is just a start," she observed at that time.[1] Even yet, even with thousands coming to Christ in revivals in 1984, and in 1985, with approximately 8,700 baptized in 1984, and with some 12,657 professions of faith in crusades in 1985, the current fuel crisis continues to thwart mobility of missionaries, and thus slow growth of baptisms and new churches in over half of the 22 associations in Tanzania.[2] Dear Lord, how much longer will many other as yet unreached tribes, as well as hundreds of thousands of tribes like them around the world, have to wait for us at home to wake up?

Writing in *The Pulpit Commentary*, E. Johnson told us that "The heathen were prepared for the gospel, all the more from the weariness and failure of their age-old 'groping after God.' "[3] So we see why it is in God's infinite plan and purpose for lost souls, even the unreached, to seek and to grope for Him, even though God knows that by their own unaided efforts lost people can never find Him. It is because the human heart must be made ready for God to make Himself known when Christian missionaries take lost ones the gospel.

Who of us Christians will introduce to them the Desire of all nations who alone can give them "beauty for ashes, the oil of joy for mourning" (Isa. 61:3)? Must they keep on reaching out for the Rock of Ages and never find Him? Who of us will tell them of the friend who sticks closer than a brother?

> Ye Christian heralds! go, proclaim
> Salvation thro' Immanuel's name;
> To distant climes the tidings bear,
> And plant the Rose of Sharon there.[4]

BOURNE HALL DRAPER

He is never far from any one of us (Acts 17:27, Beck). He will bear witness of Me (John 15:26, NASB).

6
The One Spirit Witness of the One Savior

Before a little Jew spoke to them in a hushed tone from Mars Hill, never before had the people of Athens been so snaken from head to foot. Paul led them to understand that before his coming God had never been absent from them in witness. "He is never far from any one of us since we can neither breathe, move, nor even live without Him" (paraphrase mine). Yet, as never before in their lives, each one present felt an eternal jolt. That day, through God's man each experienced God's Holy Spirit bearing witness to him of God's gospel truth concerning His Savior Son. Yet, each knew that more than a man had spoken to him that day.

Each one gave clear evidence of this in his marked reaction. All gave themselves away. Either their derisive laughter was too loud, or their attempts to put Paul off till another day was too pronounced, or else their ready acceptance of Paul's gospel was quite unmistakable. Dionysius, Damaris, and others with them bore positive evidence of the effectiveness of God's infallible Word as wielded and interpreted by His authoritative Spirit Witness. Yet, however their response, everyone present found it sharper than any double-edged sword, penetrating even to dividing soul and spirit, joints and marrow, and judging the thoughts and attitudes of their hearts. (See Heb. 4:12, NIV.)

While on earth Jesus promised to send His Holy Spirit into the world. As regarding the lost, the Spirit has come to prepare men's hearts for the gospel, to glorify the Son, to light and to guide man the way to Jesus, to regenerate all who receive the one Savior of the world. "He will bear witness of Me," Jesus foretold (John 15:26, NASB).

Now many lying spirits are gone out into the world to strive with people through false witness to lead them astray. So consider with me:

How Else Can God Strive with Lost Persons Than by His Spirit Witness?

Many false spirits inspire men to proclaim false and damning doctrines to their fellowmen. Yet God has only one Spirit Witness to lost men. Only men regenerated and indwelt by Him proclaim the truth as to salvation. How then can we tell the difference between the Spirit of truth and the spirit of error? God's Word informs us. "This is how you can recognize the Spirit of God: Every spirit that acknowledges that Jesus Christ has come in the flesh is from God, but every spirit that does not acknowledge Jesus is not from God" (1 John 4:2-2, 3 NIV).

Preaching Jesus on the day of Pentecost, Peter quoted God's promise from Joel to pour out of His Spirit upon all flesh in the last days. Ever since Adam's fall, God's Spirit has been striving with lost people through the light of nature, through the light of conscience, and—with those having them—through the light of the Scriptures. But since the coming of the gospel age, and especially since Pentecost, God's Spirit has been striving with men through Christians' proclamation of the gospel of Jesus Christ.

Jesus explained: "When he comes, he will convict the

world of guilt in regard to sin and righteousness and judgment" (John 16:8, NIV). This word *convict* is also translated "reprove" or "convince." The strongest of the three is *convince*. The Spirit convicts and reproves a sinner, so He can convince him of his absolute need of Christ as his Savior.

First, He must reveal to the sinner that he is guilty before God. He fastens the truth of the gospel upon the sinner's conscience so securely that he cannot dislodge it. So long as the striving lasts, the lost man must see himself as standing face-to-face with the righteous Son of God. Dwight L. Moody once illustrated this reality by showing how he got a similar truth across to his little boy. Having heard that a circus was in town, Moody's little son had been begging his daddy to take him that day. Moody promised him he would if he came home that afternoon and found the boy clean. But when Moody returned home, the little boy was playing in his backyard and was filthy as a pig. "Daddy, I's ready to go to the circus," Moody heard immediately. "Will you take me now?" "Now you remember what I said about you having to be clean if I took you?" his father reminded him. "Oh, yes, Daddy, but I's clean!" Moody did not argue with his little boy. He simply took him up in his arms and carried him into the house where he held him up before a big mirror and let him see himself. There is a big mirror that the Holy Spirit uses to convince sinners that they are guilty before God. That mirror is the scriptural portrayal of the person and life of Jesus Christ.

When God's Spirit causes lost man to see himself as standing face-to-face with Jesus, the way to God, the sinner knows he is in the wrong way. As face-to-face with Jesus the Truth, he knows that he is living a lie. As face-to-face with Jesus the Life, he knows he is dead in trespasses and sins. Before the Spirit showed him Jesus, he may have felt that he was guilty. Now he *knows* he is guilty, and he knows why. He knows it is because his sin has separated him from Jesus the Way, the Truth, and the Life. He knows he is separated by his own unwillingness to join in one accord with Jesus: "Of sin, because they believe not on me" (John 16:9).

Now, many lying spirits through false witness are drawing people away from the one Savior. So, again, consider with me:

How Else Can God Draw
Lost Persons to Jesus Than by His Spirit Witness?

Since more than human witness alone is required to convince lost people of their sin, so more than human power is required to draw lost people to the Savior. Billy Graham observed: "Apart from the ministry of the Holy Spirit we would never clearly see the truth of God concerning our sin, or the truth of God about our Savior. I believe this is what Jesus meant in John 6:44: 'No one can come to Me, unless the Father who sent Me draws him; and I will raise him up on the last day' " (NASB).[1]

Do you see how the Holy Spirit draws lost people to Jesus? He does it by magnifying the Savior upon the cross, dying for mankind's sin. Before the sinner's eyes He exalts Jesus' blood and righteousness. He convinces the sinner that Jesus' death in his stead is proof He loves him and is willing to forgive and save him.

Further, God's Spirit draws the lost to Jesus by lifting up before their eyes the resurrected, ascended Lord Jesus. He lets sinners see that God the Father's bringing His Son back from the horrors of death to reign at His own right hand is certain proof that Jesus' blood is God's approved remedy to relieve sinners of their sin guilt: "Of righteousness, because I go to my Father, and ye see me no more" (John 16:10).

God's Spirit not only convinces the sinner of sin and of righteousness. He also convinces the sinner of judgment. Exalting before the sinner's eyes the resurrected, reigning Lord Jesus, He shows him Jesus as victorious over Satan. Satan's power is broken. The sinner no longer needs to remain Satan's hostage. "Of judgment, because the prince of this world is judged" (John 16:11).

God's Spirit shows the sinner that God's resurrection of His Son from death is proof that God is both able and willing to resurrect the sinner from spiritual death to spiritual life. Now the sinner has no recourse. He must either rush headlong into the outstretched arms of the one Savior, or else he must turn away from God and plunge deeper into the darkness of rebellion. Dr. Graham again reminds us that "the Bible also gives us a solemn warning about resisting the calling of the Holy Spirit. In Genesis 6:3 we read: 'My Spirit shall not strive with man forever' [NASB]. Without the 'striving' of the Spirit it would be impossible for a person to come to Christ. Yet, there is also the danger that we will pass the point of no return, and that our hearts will be so calloused and hardened by sin that we will no longer hear the voice of the Spirit."[2]

Yet so long as God's Spirit Witness has the sinner under strong conviction, neither men nor devils can keep him from the realization of his spiritual death and distance from God.

All false spirits put to rout, therefore,

How Else Can God Resurrect
the Dead Sinner than by His Spirit Witness?

If no other voice than the voice of God the Son could call people, such as Lazarus, back from physical death, can any other voice than the voice of God the Spirit call the sinner forth from spiritual death to spiritual life? Only as the sinner hears and responds to the still small voice of

Jesus' Spirit can he or she experience resurrection from the darkness of death to the light of God's life. Jesus said, "The hour is coming, and now is, when the dead shall hear the voice of the Son of God: and they that hear shall live" (John 5:25). How authoritative, how powerful, how convincing is that voice!

Concerning the absolute necessity of Christian witnesses having the witness of God's Holy Spirit to give our testimony impetus unto salvation in the hearts and lives of those who hear us, Avery T. Willis, Jr., affirmed in his book *The Biblical Basis of Missions:* "The lordship of Christ gives the believer *authority* to bear witness to everyone. The presence of the Holy Spirit gives him the spiritual *ability* to make an impact on those hearing the testimony. The Spirit-filled believer never witnesses alone. The Holy Spirit works within the lost person to verify and to personalize the witness of the believer. He makes real the authority and the presence of Christ.

"To witness without the power of the Holy Spirit is folly. . . . God's mission demands God's power."[3]

God's promise of the outpouring of His Spirit in great witnessing power is for any church anywhere, any time during the last days. (See Joel 2:28-32; Acts 2:16 ff; especially v. 39.) Yet to have this power given, a church must claim it by all-out surrender and faith.

I know a country church near where I live that claimed God's promise of outpouring. Nestled among the ridges of Lee County in Southwest, Virginia, Friendship Baptist Church was the church of my mother's parents, brothers and sisters, and where my dear mother herself found Christ at the age of eleven. Here I can first remember my parents taking me to church as a small child. Over the years, Friendship has prayed down the old-time power again and again, but to my knowledge never more so than some five years ago.

A young evangelist named Ronnie Owens, pastor at Silver Leaf, was called to preach in a revival scheduled for one week. I had asked Ronnie to preach in a revival to begin the week following in the church I was pastoring at the time. But Saturday night preceding the Sunday beginning our revival, Ronnie called me on the phone.

"Jimmy, I sure hate not to keep my appointment with you folks, but God is blessing so much here at Friendship I just can't leave yet. Lost people are flooding down the aisles every service. While the Spirit is moving so, I dare not leave."

"Of course, you must not leave there now, Ronnie," I replied; "I'll preach in my own revival."

Sunday night after his service, Ronnie called me again, telling how the people were still coming to Christ in significant numbers. Monday night, Tuesday night, Wednesday night, and Thursday night he called to say there was no letup in sight. Friday night following his service he called to tell me that he had only been able to preach for about fifteen minutes when lost people interrupted his sermon by beginning to pour down the aisles under heavy conviction. Both Protestants and Catholics who had thought themselves saved were discovering their lost condition and flocking to the Savior. At the conclusion of this two-weeks outpouring, some 120 or more decisions had been registered, around 60 being first-time professions of faith. After the God-honoring baptismal service, the membership of Friendship had more than doubled. Now the beautiful new church they have erected nearby is much larger than the old church and continues to grow. All praise to the God of promise!

As to our utter dependence upon the power of God's Spirit Witness to win in the crucial battle over the false witness of satanic spirits in the hearts of unbelievers, Willis further emphasized: "The Holy Spirit works throughout the world to prepare men's hearts for the gospel, but his primary work among God's people is to send them forth with the gospel message. To march into the battle without the guidance of the Spirit is as foolish as an army's marching into battle without a general. For us to testify of God's grace without the power of the Holy Spirit is to fight without weapons. Satan, the evil spirit, fights for control over the lives of those whom he has seduced. His grip can be broken only by the power of the Holy Spirit. The Spirit works through God's people to accomplish his mission."[4]

Who alone can convert the sinner who is both convicted of his sin and convinced of his need of Jesus? God's Spirit Witness. Through the miracle of regeneration He imparts to the sinner the very nature of God instantaneously the very day that he believes the Voice he hears.

Along with his tribe, an African chief was hearing the gospel for the first time. Unlike too many gospel-hardened Americans who insist that the preacher conclude his sermon on the very last minute of the hour, these gospel-famished Africans kept imploring the American missionaries to tell them the wonderful story of Jesus and His redeeming love again and again that same day.

As the impassive chief leaned back against a rear tent pole and rested the long handle of his spear on the ground, one of the weary but delighted missionary preachers would end his sermon with an invitation to accept the Savior. Each time, a number would come forward evidently touched profoundly. Then, bone-tired and ready for a rest, the missionaries would wait for the sizable crowd to disperse, so they could retire to their living quarters. But each time as they started to move away, many eager faces would surround them. Every way they turned, they would confront ivory-white teeth gleaming in smiles and bright, hungry eyes burning deep into their souls. "Please tell us more about Jesus!" they would hear many voices pleading. "Please preach to us about Jesus. We've never heard of anyone like Him before."

The shadows lengthened and softened the sweltering, equatorial day into soothing night as the missionaries continued to preach while the chief listened intently but distantly. At the conclusion of each message when more weeping people would respond, the missionaries would covertly watch the chief. They sought to see whether God's double-edged sword as wielded by His Spirit Witness was having effect upon him. But if the chief were moved at all they could not tell it.

Finally, a little after midnight there was a commotion at the back. Men, women, and children were scurrying right and left. His face sober in the midst of his grand regalia, and as outwardly inexpressive as ever, the stalwart chief was coming to the front. Decisively confronting the preacher, he gave him his hand and sank down on one knee. "Great Witness has spoken to chief tonight," he acknowledged. "Chief would be most ungracious if he did not answer with himself, his all."

Certainly, this is what God's unseen Spirit Witness can do in one day. But what of the many chiefs and their tribes of the world who have never heard the voice of God's Spirit witnessing through the preached Word even for the first time?

We want to know, therefore, what these things mean (Acts 17:20, NASB).

7
Multitudes Without the One-Spirit Witness

While it is true that we Christians cannot witness without the Spirit, I believe it is equally true that the Spirit cannot witness the gospel without us Christians. In many passages, as well as in its total context, the Bible makes it clear that no sinner can be won to Christ without one or more Christian witnesses through whom God's one Spirit Witness can deal with him.

Do you think that unless Paul or some other Christian had witnessed to the Athenians any one of them could have been won? Impossible. Even when they had heard Paul witnessing in the public square, they desired a more detailed explanation.

Let us examine the record and ask,

How Else Can God's Spirit Strive with Sinners Than Through Our Christian Testimony?

I challenge anybody to produce scriptural or historical evidence that God has ever converted a sinner without the testimony of a redeemed sinner. Examine the Bible record. See if you can find any such instance. When for one hundred and twenty years God's Spirit strove with the antediluvians, through what means did He strive? Why, through the preaching of Noah. When God's Spirit won the city of Nineveh, through what means did he win the city? Why, through the testimony of Jonah.

Even when God speaks to lost persons through dreams or visions, He still requires another person who has experienced the new birth to witness the gospel to them before He converts them. Joas Maxima de Oliveria, who was one of the participants in Operation Transtotal—an intensive program of Brazilian Baptists in 1978 to evangelize the many new colonists along the Trans-Amazon Highway—told of such a dream: "It was 3:00 p.m. when, after walking eight kilometers, we entered into the last house in our section to be visited that day.

"As we arrived," he continued, "a crude looking young man, but one who needed Jesus, came to the door and invited us in. Even before we had finished talking to him about the love of God in Christ, he, very touched and moved by the Holy Spirit, said, 'Look, young man, three days ago I dreamed that a group of Christians had come here to speak to me about Christ. I said to my wife that we needed to change.'

"We continued to explain to him the plan of God for our salvation, and he accepted Jesus. The Holy Spirit, in reality, went before us preparing hearts," concluded Joas.[1]

Does this remind you of the way God spoke to and won Cornelius, the Roman centurion? See Acts 10 and 11. God confronted this devout man in a vision. Cornelius saw and heard speaking one of God's resplendent angels. But did God convert Cornelius by the testimony of His angel? By no means. Why not? No angel has ever been lost in sin and redeemed by the blood of the Crucified One. A mortal man who had been lost in sin and so redeemed had to be sent for. Not until the arrival and testimony of the apostle Peter could Cornelius experience true salvation.

When Jesus declared to His first apostles, "Ye shall receive power, after that the Holy Ghost is come upon you:

and ye shall be witnesses unto me both in Jerusalem, and in all Judaea, and in Samaria, and unto the uttermost part of the earth" (Acts 1:8), not only was He setting forth an invariable commission, but likewise, an invariable principle. God the Spirit's one way of witnessing to sinners is through Christian testimony.

Now let us examine the facts and ask,

How Else Can God's Spirit Draw Sinners Than Through Our Christian Influence?

More than a Christian's verbal testimony is required to work salvation in the life of a sinner. The testimony of a Christlike influence is likewise required. The sinner cannot see the ascended and invisible Christ. He must have the concrete evidence of a Christlike Christian. Paul told the Corinthians, "You yourselves are our letter, written on our hearts, known and read by everybody. You show that you are a letter from Christ, the result of our ministry, written not with ink but with the Spirit of the living God, not on tablets of stone but on tablets of human hearts" (2 Cor. 3:2-3, NIV).

Do you suppose the Athenians would ever have been moved as they were by the truth of the gospel Paul preached if first they had not been deeply impressed by Paul's Christlike conduct and Christlike attitude? Very likely Paul's Christlike influence, just as much as his bringing strange ideas to their ears, led them to insist, "We want to know therefore what these things mean" (Acts 17:20, NASB). First of all, Paul's personal life must be written upon their hearts. Then they were ready to hear what he had to say. Before sinners can be told "what these things mean," they must be shown "what these things mean."

Before the sinner can understand how Jesus could become obedient even unto death, he must first see us

Christians living in all-out submission to our Father God. Before the sinner can understand Jesus' compassion, he must first encounter Christian compassion. He must first observe Christians living in one accord, mutual tolerance, and brotherly love. He must first observe Christian concern for him. "By this shall all men know," Jesus emphasized. (See John 13:35.)

But I hear someone asking, "What about billions who have never heard of Jesus? They have never heard of us Christians, either, have they? So how can we influence them for good or bad?" Well, even when Christians fly high above them in airplanes and drop them gospel messages, they must sense the godly compassion of these unknowns. Even when Christians preach the gospel to these billions by radio, they must sense the godly concern of these they've never met.

Yet what about billions more who have neither received gospel literature nor heard gospel broadcasts: Are they without Christian influence altogether? Well, don't you imagine that they often wonder why someone does not come and explain to them what mean these things they perceive of Deity from the lights of nature and conscience?

So let us examine reality and ask,

How Else Can God's Spirit Convert Sinners Than Through Our Christian Instrumentality?

It is marvelous that many lost pagans are reached and won through gospel literature distribution and broadcasts. Still, indisputably, many other individuals who read such literature and hear such broadcasts very definitely need some ambassador of Christ present to explain to them face-to-face what these things mean. If many who answer the invitation in American gospel meetings need a personal explanation to help them understand, how much more do many who hear the gospel for the first time?

Where would the Ethiopian official have been without Phillip? Where would he be today? What if Phillip had not been in the Spirit when the Lord commanded him to go down to Samaria and lead the Samaritans in that great revival? Then he would not have been there when the Spirit later ordered him south to the road leading from Jerusalem to Gaza, would he? Then he would not have been at the right place at the right time to hear the Spirit directing him to the Ethiopian's chariot. Then he would not have found the official reading from Isaiah 53. Then he would not have been on hand when the official desperately needed some helpful Christian to ask, "Do you understand what you are reading?" Does the Ethiopian's reply, "How can I unless someone explains it to me?" (Acts 8:30-31, NIV) mean to you that this man could not have been saved without the help of Phillip or some other Christian? But for Phillip would this man now be in hell? What then of the Ethiopian church that tradition tells us the official returned to his homeland and founded? What then of his entire nation?

Lost multitudes are now waiting for some Christian to bring them the gospel and then explain to them what these things mean. There with them is God's Spirit Witness waiting. G. Campbell Morgan asserted that "The Holy Spirit is waiting in the far-distant places of the earth for the voice of anointed man to preach, in order that through that instrumentality He may carry on His work of convicting of sin, and of righteousness, and of judgment."[2]

Of earth's billions only we Christians have God's Spirit Witness within. All others have Him all about them and as near as life itself. Nevertheless, He is outside their hearts. They thirst for Him, having "Water, water everywhere, Nor any drop to drink."[3] How can they invite him inside to quench their thirst except "some man should guide" them? How wide is the gap between them and the Spirit! That gap only we Christians can fill. Of course, Christ is the one Mediator, but the gap between them and Christ's Spirit Witness is the gap that only we Christians can fill. Have you ever heard God's still small voice whisper to you, "I sought for a man . . . that should . . . stand in the gap . . . but I found none" (Ezek. 22:30)? Fellow Christians, we must fill that gap at once.

Do not count me among those who contend that after our Lord has returned for His church and taken us Christians all home with Him, many will still be converted. Dr. Oswald J. Smith explained how this idea is neither logical nor scriptural: "But I know what some are saying. I hear it everywhere. They are saying: 'This is not the task of the Church at all. The Jews are to do it; we should leave it for them after we have been raptured away.'

"I know of no theory that can do more to cut the nerve of missionary endeavor. Moreover, I know of no definite statement in the entire Bible that would lead me to believe, for one single moment, that the Jews are to evangelize the world during the days of the great tribulation, as some people seem to think. Were I to believe that, I would fold my arms and do nothing.

"Do you mean to say that after the Holy Spirit has gone, and we are told that He is to go when the Church goes, do you mean to say that the Jews can accomplish more in some seven years or less, without the help of the Holy Spirit, in the midst of persecution and martyrdom, than we have been able to accomplish in nearly two thousand years, with the Holy Spirit's aid, when it has been easy to be a Christian? Preposterous! Impossible!

"Furthermore, if nothing is to be done until the Church has been raptured, then only that one generation, the generation that will be living during the tribulation, will ever be evangelized. Are you willing then that every other generation should perish? Have you no concern for your own generation? Are we going to allow this generation to be lost and be satisfied if the last generation only is evangelized? Paul's burden was for the first generation of the Christian era.

"Even if you are right, still I am going to do all I can, because the job has to be done sometime. Everyone agrees on that. Well, then, the more I can do now the less the Jews will have to do then. But if you are wrong, what a tragedy! You will have failed to do your part to evangelize the world, and God will hold you responsible. I believe it must be done now."[4]

I ask you, fellow Christian, to face with me this pertinate question: Does God's Spirit Witness ever win souls independently of us Christians? No more than we Christians will ever be able to win souls independently of Him. Was old John Collett Ryland, the hyper-Calvinist, correct when he snapped at William Carey's insistence that Christ's Great Commission to His apostles is obligatory on all succeeding ministers to the end of the world: "Young man, sit down! When God pleases to convert the heathen, he will do it without your aid or mine"[5]? If not, then must we not conclude that Carey was correct?

Then if Carey is correct, is he not correct because 1 Corinthians 3:9 states the major premise of the inescapable responsibility of every one of us Christians in this matter of world missions: "We are labourers together with God"? Having then this foundational truth, can we be true Christians unless we stand to our feet on it with Carey and join him in his interpretation of Isaiah 54:2-3 when he preached in the spring of 1792 at Notingham, hammering home his two immortal points: "Expect great things from God; attempt great great things for God"?

God . . . now commandeth all men everywhere to repent (Acts 17:30).

8
God's One Plan for Everyone

"How is Christianity superior to any other world religion?" the college student asked me. "In England all roads lead to London. So won't one religion, as well as another, lead you where you need to go now, and to heaven at last—if you're sincere in what you believe?"

"Certainly not," I answered. "All religions other than Christianity are devious ways. They cannot satisfy in this life. Together they form the broad way that leads to hell ultimately. There is only one way that provides life fulfillment now and leads to heaven at last. That way is the straight and narrow way that Jesus taught. In fact, Jesus declared, 'I am the way.' Christianity is superior because it is the way of the one true God."

"Aw, come off it!" objected the college man. "Just who is to say what one way is superior? Truth is relative. Truth is subjective. What is truth for you may not be truth for me. Who's to really say what is the one absolute? On whose authority is your way the one straight and narrow?"

"On whose authority is truth relative?" I countered. "Any truth is narrow. Try changing the laws of mathematics or the laws of chemistry, for example. On the authority of His Godhead, Jesus narrowed the truth to Himself. He says, 'I am the way, the truth, and the life: no man cometh unto the Father, but by me' (John 14:6).

"To me, truth is Jesus Christ living inside me. He has proved Himself to me by making me alive from spiritual death, and by giving me life that is abundant and meaningful."

"How do you know you that you are alive from the dead? Prove to me that Jesus is who He claims to be."

"That I cannot do."

"Oh-ho!"

"No man can prove Jesus to another man. But if you will simply invite Jesus into your heart by faith, He will prove Himself to you personally as He has proved Himself to countless believers around the world, even many hearing of Him for the first time. Isn't it strange that you who have heard the gospel so many times are so hard to convince while many who hear for the first time accept Jesus without question?"

Come now, let's be reasonable. Besides Christianity,

What Other Religion Has a Plan for the Salvation of the Human Soul?

Other religions have plans to escape suffering, to achieve reincarnation, and so forth, but these are man's own plans to save himself. Not one of them gives satisfaction. Only by His own plan does God give both salvation from sin and a satisfactory answer to the human identity question: "Who am I?" Only by His own plan does God give man an answer to who he is in relationship to the Divine Being he knows must be, and who he is to God for all time and eternity.

Then listen, all mankind, for the God of all the earth is speaking: "O earth, earth, earth, hear the word of the Lord" (Jer. 22:29). When the first man fell, God came walking in the cool of the day and calling, "Adam

. . . where art thou?" (Gen. 3:9). So whoever you are, wherever you are in the earth, the God who knows all about you is now calling your name and demanding of you an accounting of your whereabouts in your relationship to Him.

But most of earth's inhabitants do not hear God's call. They are not tuned in to God's frequency. Were their ears not so dull of hearing, they would hear God's call to all mankind as sounded forth by Paul from the court of Areopagus: "God . . . now commandeth all men everywhere to repent."

God's universal call to repentance is His call to accept His one plan of salvation for everyone everywhere. It is His call to a realization of Jesus' name as the only name under heaven whereby we must be saved. Before anyone can experience this great salvation, he must repent toward its Author.

Multitudes of the lost today know they have transgressed against their own consciences, against their fellowmen, even against Deity, known or unknown. But only when in confrontation with the scriptural Godhead does a person face up to the seriousness of his sin. Only then does he hear God asking, "What have you done?" (Gen. 4:10, NIV). Only then comes his reply, "I have failed to measure up to Jesus Christ, God's exacting plumb line of the universe. By refusing Jesus' death as my atonement, I have betrayed the innocent blood!" Therefore, in His call to repentance God is bidding everyone to a reckoning. Man must reckon with his Maker and Redeemer either now or at the judgment. God would have it now while there is still time for people to settle their differences with their God.

God's universal call to repentance is His call to a recognition of the universal and absolute necessity of the conversion of the total person. Jesus called it the new birth.

No other religion recognizes the necessity of the new birth. Why? No otner religion has any clear conception of the true God and His Son and, consequently, no clear conception of sin. Only when in confrontation with God by the Holy Spirit's conviction, does man realize that without holiness no one shall see the Lord. (See Heb. 12:14.) Then man knows that his moral and spiritual pollution must be cleansed. Then he knows that something must be done about his unclean record. He knows that something must be done about his unclean daily habits. He knows that something must be done about his unclean nature.

Then man knows that he must be made a new creation in Christ Jesus. He recognizes the utter change that he must undergo to dwell with the all-holy God. Likewise he recognizes his own utter impotence to change himself.

Here stands the stupendous contrast between Christianity and all other religions. Christianity alone has a Christ able to save unto the uttermost, that is, completely. By His death, burial, and resurrection Christ alone has done everything that needs to be done to effect man's salvation. Since His atonement is once and for all for sin, Jesus is able to transform one's soul, life, and destiny once and for all. All other religions are full of man's endless efforts to lift himself by his own bootstraps. Man must make himself acceptable to his conception of Deity.

But only in confrontation with the God of the Bible does man become so aware of his own state of helplessness that he realizes he can do nothing whatsoever either to save himself or to assist God in saving him. Only thus do humans see the futility of their inflicting punishment upon themselves for their sins. Now they know that they must have Jesus' atonement. Only thus do humans see the futility of their performing good works. Now they know that they must have Jesus' righteousness imputed to them. Only thus do humans see the futility of their doing penance. Now they know that they must exercise repentance.

Lost ones must see that their sin—having put Christ to death—is red like crimson, that their rejection of Jesus is deep-dyed scarlet. Then they will distinctly hear God's still small voice require of them, "Why have ye done this?" (Judg. 2:2). Then lost ones will cry out in agony of soul, "What must I do to be saved?" (Acts 16:30).

Then, and only then, will lost persons hear God give them His one plan for every human being. They must repent toward God and call upon the Lord Jesus Christ in saving faith. If they do, God will wash them white as snow. (See Acts 20:21; Isa. 1:18.) Therefore, in His call to repentance, God is calling everyone everywhere to a reasoning.

"I say, that's quite a reasoning for God to be calling all people to, and over half of humankind not even aware of it!" you may be exclaiming. It is, indeed!

Sharpen your wits, humanity. Besides Christianity,

What Other Religion Has a Plan
for the Fulfillment of Our Lives

Visit the non-Christian shrines and temples of this earth. Do you find the faces of the worshipers smiling or downcast? Visit Red Russia or Red China. Visit the Muslim countries. What is it you read in the faces of the majority of the people? Where is the spring in their step? Where is their joy? Where is their sense of fulfillment?

Only in the faces of those who know Jesus Christ do we find genuine rapture. Only in their lives do we discover a sense of lasting fulfillment. Only when we can say with Paul, "For to me to live is Christ," are we really living the abundant life Jesus has for all who will follow Him in all-out allegiance. (See Phil. 1:21.)

In His call to repentance God is calling every human being everywhere to life fulfillment.

Think of all that human potential for God's glory being wasted! Every man, woman, boy, and girl alive is created full of potential for God's service and use. There are no exceptions. There is no "dull, ignorant heathen" incapable of valuable development spiritually, once his or her resources have been unleashed by the new birth. If Africans just out of the bush can be taught in short order to fly modern jets, what can they be taught to perform in the spiritual diminsion? Any one of thousands of missionaries can tell you from firsthand observation on the field.

I once met an Aborigine from the Australian outback who had been converted to Christ. His English name is Peter. I thrilled with wonder as I heard Peter tell a group of American Christians of his life before and after he met Jesus. He had lived the primitive, almost subhuman existence of the typical aboriginal wanderer, subsisting on snakes, snails, kangaroos, and very little water. Totally illiterate and ignorant of the one true God, he had lived as a pagan.

Then, wandering one day near the white man's civilization, he came upon a Christian mission station. The women missionaries invited Peter to stay with them and attend their school. But first, they insisted that he take a bath. Once alone in the bathroom Peter was nonplused at the sight of a whole tub full of water. He had never had a bath before in his life. The women finally discovered that the bathroom window was up, and Peter was gone.

Months later, having rejoined a group of fellow Aborigine youths who wandered from place to place like a pack of Dingo dogs, Peter and the others came again into the outskirts of the city where the mission station was. Yet for days they avoided going into the station. During this time, being famished and finding nothing else to eat, they caught, killed, and devoured an alley cat.

At last Peter ventured again to the doors of the mission station. Again he found himself more than welcome. The women had been grieving over him and praying for his return. Moreover, they had been praying for his soul's salvation. Peter wasn't sure what all this meant, but he was convinced they loved him with a love he had never known before. So this time he remained to attend both their Christian school and their Christian services. It wasn't long until Peter accepted Jesus Christ as his own personal Savior. After this, his life really began to change.

I would like for all the world to see Peter as he is today. I would love for all to hear him play so beautifully "Count Your Many Blessings," blowing through his fingers on a leaf from a tree. I would love for all to hear him play his guitar and sing, "No One Ever Cared for Me Like Jesus." Above all, I wish the whole world could look into Peter's transformed face. I felt sure I saw Jesus with the light of the glory of God upon his face that day. It was in the black, radiant face of Peter that I saw Jesus.

Yet how can lost multitudes, who are still as lost as Peter once was, glorify God and His Son with their lives, or find life fulfillment when they have never even heard of God or His Son?

Think long, world. Except for Christianity,

What Other Religion Has a Plan for the Realization of Man's Destiny?

What is the Christian faith? It is Christ in us, the hope of glory. (See Col. 1:27.) It is for us to live in Jesus, and for Jesus to live in us now and forevermore. For us to live is Christ, and to die is gain. (See Phil. 1:21.) It is for us to rejoice in God and in His Son now and throughout eternity. It is for us to serve our Lord in this life and in the new heavens and the new earth, world without end. It is for us, the redeemed, to live in never-ceasing love, fellowship, and blessed one accord with one another and with our great God.

By what other faith can one reach heaven to meet God face-to-face and find oneself faultless before the presence of His glory with exceeding joy? (See Jude 24.) By what other faith can individuals, having gained heaven, look back over their lives on earth and glory in the fact that they have lived life for God's pleasure in the fulfillment of His will, plan, and purpose? By what other faith can individuals, having gotten to heaven, look forward to an eternity of living in perfect accord with God's will, plan, and purpose for them?

Does God actually have such a unique plan for every living man, woman, and child? Most assuredly. In His universal call to repentance, God is calling every person everywhere to the realization of their destiny. Why, then, are the many not in on it? As you know, many have heard much of it but think little of it. Billions more have never even heard that God is calling them. Don't you think it's time we confront them with God's one plan for every human being? Isn't it time we confront with a fuller explanation of God's one plan the many others who, while they may have heard, have not yet had an adequate opportunity to respond to the claims of the gospel? David M. Howard, general director of World Evangelical Fellowship, wrote me that he and many other missiologists now number the lost as being in the neighborhood of 3 billion people in a world population of approximately 4.8 billion[1]? [As this book was being edited, we were told that the world's population had reached 5 billion.]

Again and again we keep hearing this three billion figure from missiologist after missiologist, and from Christian world leader after Christian world leader. Have you stopped to think how many unreached people that is? Thirty hundred million! Where, in your thinking, are these thirty hundred million unreached human souls? When you consider your Lord, do you think of those thirty hundred million out there who are right now groping all alone in their darkness without Him?

Why has God left you and me here on earth? Why hasn't He taken us on to that far better place called heaven? Why has God placed untold resources in our hands, abundant talents in our keeping, and precious time at our disposal? Doesn't He mean for us to use what He has given us for His glory? How else can we do that than first upon our knees, then upon our abilities, then upon our financial means, and all the while upon our feet advancing, ever advancing in step with the ever-advancing Redeemer in the direction of those thirty hundred million, as well as the many all about us who have heard but not responded, those thirty hundred million who either have yet to hear or yet to hear clearly, and to have an adequate opportunity to respond to God's one plan for every person?

We can all go upon our knees daily, joining hands with the more than 200,000 Southern Baptists here in our homeland who have committed themselves to pray each day for specific prayer requests related to foreign missions; we can all go around the world day after day praying for the countries of our world with their teeming masses of individuals who need to hear, or hear again, God's one plan of salvation. Upon our knees "we become vessels for God's use, focusing His power and purpose wherever God's servants are telling His story."[2] Upon our feet utilizing our abilities, our means, and our time we become God's only means of reaching the unreached. God has placed the money in our hands. He has placed the world in our hearts. He has given us a responsive, dangerous, and opportune moment in history. He is loving us to love a lost world.

FOREIGN MISSIONS IS KEEPING THE WORLD IN VIEW—AND MORE.

We Southern Baptists have committed ourselves to a cause far beyond our individual awareness. That's what Bold Mission Thrust is all about: a vision of a world where every person may hear and respond to the answer to all their questions and longings—Jesus Christ.

It is a vision based on love and trust. The cause is humanity-wide. It is God-sized.[3]

9
Untold Masses Ignorant of God's One Plan

In his day Robert Moffat said of Africa, "I have looked at the smoke rising from a thousand villages where the gospel has never been preached." Quoting these words that stirred the heart of David Livingstone, R. Keith Parks, president of our Southern Baptist Foreign Mission Board, said of Africa in our day, "When I visited West Africa in April, I saw the smoke of ten thousand villages—all in one great city.

Whether the place is Dakar, Senegal; or Abidjan, Ivory Coast; or Accra, Ghana; or Lagos, Nigeria, more people who have never heard the gospel cluster in one city than would have been in the ten thousand villages Moffat saw.

As I looked at these cities, the experience of Jesus weeping over Jerusalem came again and again to my mind and heart. Some of today's cities seem almost without hope; their people strongly resist the gospel. Other cities show overwhelming response. If we could find the best ways and had just a few more people to mobilize the emerging African leadership, some of these great cities would see tens of thousands come to Christ.

Never in history have so many people been gathered so tightly together. This offers unprecedented opportunity to win many to Jesus Christ. We as Southern Baptists must do our part in sharing the gospel with the cities of all the

world, not just in Africa. Worldwide, we work in at least 40 cities of more than one million people. . . .
We have not, and we will not, forget the villages. But we must do more for the cities, as we keep the world in view.[1]

The cry of lost billions around the world ought to stir our Christian hearts today as the cry of those Moffat referred to stirred the heart of Livingstone. Many people who are unaware of God's one plan for everyone have heard *of* it, but they still do not know what it is. Even as the citizens of Athens implored Paul, these many cry aloud to us Christians today, "Come and tell us more about this new religion" (TLB). Many more than these have never heard of God's one plan even once. Even more pathetic is their cry, "Come and tell us"!

I ask you now, my fellow believer,

Unless We Christians Hear Their Cry to Hear, Must Billions Remain Without Direction?

Even as the plea of the Athenians in Paul's day comes the plea of multitudes in our day, "May we know . . .?" Until now they have relied upon tradition handed down to them, upon the speculation of religious leaders, upon mere opinion, upon human theory. What they long for is certainty. How often must they wonder, "Is there such a thing as sure knowledge?"

Consider them there in their trackless desert. Forever they drift. Forever they wander, further and further from the truth. Surrounded by a horizon full of directions, they do not know which direction to take. Their understanding is befuddled. Paul wrote of the Gentiles as walking "in the vanity of their mind, Having the understanding darkened, being alienated from the life of God through the ignorance that is in them, because of the blindness of their heart" (Eph. 4:17-18). Their cry comes to us today: "May we know which direction to go to find the right way? Can all of these directions be right? If not, then which one of them is the right direction?" They are begging for someone who knows to come and tell them.

"May we know what to do to appease and to please the Great One or Ones? Must we forever worship in ignorance? We are confused." That cry is one of bewilderment and desperation. In *The Pulpit Commentary*, R. Tuck described this confusion, particularly that of polytheism: "Its worshippers can never be quite sure that they have propitiated the right god, seeing that gods are supposed to be related to particular places, nations, events, sins, etc. This confusion tends to create a more and more elaborate ritual, and a wearisome round of ceremonies. All gods who may possibly be related to the matter in hand must be propitiated, and then the right one may be missed."[2]

Like too many Jews, a world of aimless Gentiles "have a zeal of God, but not according to knowledge. For they being ignorant of God's righteousness, and going about to establish their own righteousness, have not submitted themselves unto the righteousness of God" (Rom. 10:2-3). How can they submit until they hear of Him who is the righteousness of God? Only by the righteous Son can they submit.

Many having heard of our gospel beg to know its contents. Their cry is: "May we know what this new teaching of yours really is?" (Phillips). Many others, having heard of Jesus, cry aloud to learn just who He is, and if He really cares for them. Their plea is, "May we know who He is who will hear us and help us?"

"May we know?" they importune us who know Jesus. "Shall you deny us knowledge of the truth perpetually? Must we forever wander directionless?"

Do you ever hear their cry? In the middle of the night do you ever wake up and hear them begging, "Come over . . . and help us"? (See Acts 16:9.) What if the apostle Paul had not first heard and then answered the Macedonian call? Would the Athenians ever have heard his gospel? What of all Europe? Would anyone else have taken these people the gospel in their day? A big question. But as for you, when you are all alone in a secluded place, with the grandeur of nature all about, do you ever feel God so near that you hear the cry of lost multitudes begging to hear the gospel? Unless we Christians hear them, how shall they hear of Jesus?

In Romans 10:14, hear Paul ask, "How then shall they call on him in whom they have not believed? and how shall they believe in him of whom they have not heard?"

Must the paths of of the lost have forever drawn across them the line of confusion? (See Isa. 34:11c.)

I ask you further, my fellow saint,

Unless We Christians Answer Their Cry, Must Billions Never Find Life Fulfillment?

Evident in their cry is their need to hear, their desire to hear, and their right to hear.

You agree with me that faith is indispensable to salvation (Heb. 11:6), and you agree that faith comes only by hearing (Rom. 10:17). Then must you not consistently agree that until or unless people hear, they are surely lost? If your loved one who has heard the gospel countless times but has not yet responded by faith is definitely lost and in desperate need, is that one far away in the regions beyond who has seldom if ever heard not definitely lost and in desperate need also? There is a difference, too often, yes.

Too often the difference is that while our lost loved ones at home keep stopping their ears so they will not have the annoyance of having to hear the gospel "crammed down their throats" again and again, the poor souls far away who are lost in ignorance keep straining their throats with their repeated cries, "Come and tell us more about this new religion" (TLB).

In the cry of the lost world there is outspoken eagerness, manifestation of burning desire, disclosure of craving thirst, and unmistakable readiness to hear. All they need is for some ambassador of Christ to come and tell them of the good news.

It was the time of Easter vacation at a famous Southern resort town. A witness for Jesus was standing at an intersection handing out tracts on God's plan of salvation. Thousands of college students from many locations of our country were filing past. I watched almost every student take the offered message, whether politely or indifferently. Then I noticed that in most every instance the student would give the tract a few cursory glances, then promptly discard it. Presently, the sidewalks and streets all about were literally blanketed with God's gospel of His Son, thrown down and trampled under hurrying feet. Heavy disfiguring shoe prints ground God's loving message into unreadability.

Come with me now to any one of the dark places of this earth. Watch with me a Christian handing out God's plan of salvation. Witness the glut of humanity surrounding the Christian. See the burning eyes. See the hungry hands straining to obtain a tract. In the regions beyond almost never does one see a gospel message thrown down or discarded. On the contrary, one sees God's plan for every human being devoured by starving hearts.

My fellow believer, don't you agree that the lost have a right to hear? Then, shall we tell them, or shall we deny them their right? Dr. Baker James Cauthen, then executive director of our Foreign Mission Board, summed up the purpose of Bold Mission Thrust at the Astrodome in Houston during the 1979 session of the Southern Baptist Convention:

Ask me what is the most basic, fundamental, urgent human right and I will answer without a shadow of being afraid that I am wrong: the basic human right of a person born into this world—with all of its sorrow and all of its potential for good or evil, and facing a river called death and eternity—his basic human right is to hear the truth of the love of God made manifest in Jesus Christ our Savior; to hear it and to respond to it for time and eternity.[3]

I ask you, my brother, my sister, ought not the cry of the lost to hear the good news move us to volunteer as Isaiah did? When in his vision of God, and of himself, Isaiah saw likewise a vision of his perishing fellow humanity, he cried out promptly, "Here am I; send me" (Isa. 6:8*d*). Shouldn't we Christians volunteer take the gospel to perishing humanity? Shouldn't we volunteer to go and tell them, either in person, in prayerful intercession, or in financial support of those who go in person, however the Lord our God sends us to them?

When at times you feel Jesus especially close, are you willing to go in person, or however your Lord sees fit to send you? If so, well and good. If not, though Jesus may in truth be close to you, are you absolutely sure you are close to Jesus? Are you positive that you are actually in step with Jesus? If we are in step with Jesus, and expect to stay in step, we had better be prepared to go to the ends of the earth, because that's where Jesus is going.

Look at Romans 10 again and hear Paul say further: "And how shall they hear without a preacher?" (v. 14).

Must the paths of the lost have forever strewn across them the stones of emptiness? (See Isa. 34:11*c.*)

I ask you finally, my fellow Christian,

Unless We Churches Send Them Missionaries, Must Billions Forever Miss Heaven?

Must the lost lift up their eyes in hell, being in torments, and see heaven only afar off? The sparkle of its water of life forever missed? The luscious fruit of its tree of life forever beyond their reach? Its joy everlastingly gone from them? Its laughter too far off ever to lift them? Its Bright and Morning Star never to rise with healing and health upon them? As John Greenleaf Whittier wrote of Maud Muller, must this be their cry for eternity?

> For of all sad words of tongue or pen,
> The saddest are these: "It might have been!"

And why, my fellow Christian? In God's name, why? Because, like many in enlightened countries of the world, they heard the gospel innumerable times, but again and again took it ever so lightly? No, my brother, my sister. Because there was no atonement provision actually made for them? No; Jesus died for all the world. Because there were no gates of heaven once open towards their ends of the earth? No; the Word of God speaks of three gates being open toward the East, three gates open toward the North, three gates open toward the South, and three gates open toward the West. None of these. But because no one ever told them of Jesus, the Way to God, the Way to heaven. No Christian ever heard their cry in time to tell them. No church ever saw the vision of their lostness in time to send them missionaries.

Must the traveled paths of millions lead to that uncrossable gulf? (See Luke 16:26.)

On a cleared plateau high in the mountains of Central Asia, natives of a certain tribe may be seen waiting, their eyes trained upon the sky in intense expectancy, hour after hour, day after day. Having for years observed what to them is the profound phenomenon of airplanes traversing the sky, and never having seen an airplane close at hand, these natives have for long concluded that the planes are giant birds bearing messages from the Great One to all peoples of the earth. For decades now they have kept prepared a crude landing strip on which they wait daily, hoping, always hoping, that one day one of the giant birds will land on their strip of earth. On that day they believe that they will receive the message from the Great One. This message, they believe, will mean everything to them. It will mean the way to peace with the Great One. When, oh when, will some gospel plane, bearing gospel missionaries, land on their strip of earth?

The God who made the world ... does not dwell in temples made with hands; ... as though He needed anything (Acts 17:24-25, NASB). There is one body (Eph. 4:4).

10
The Lord's One Body— Still Incomplete

As Paul told the worldly wise men in Athens, the Lord does not dwell in man-made edifices. Our Lord is building His own temple. This temple our Lord also calls His church, His bride, His body. And though Paul does not mention the Lord's church body in his Mars' Hill sermon since he is speaking to unconverted people, he deals at length with the concept in his various letters to churches, especially in regard to the one church universal in the Books of Ephesians and Colossians—Ephesians centering on God's purpose for His church.

In Ephesians, Paul further unfolds the plan set forth by our Lord Jesus when He declared in Caesarea Philippi, "Upon this rock" (that is, upon Himself, His atonement, His teachings, and the believer's faith in the same) "I will build my church" (Matt. 16:18). Our Lord, then, is the one doing the building. Yet He is using us who believe in Him not only as His building block units but also as His hands, His feet, His means of building, in the sense of adding new members.

The word *ekklesia* our Lord used in reference to His church body in Matthew 16:18 and 18:17 means a "called-out" body of believers, called out of a meaningless existence in the sin and death of the world, and, as Paul brings out most vividly in Ephesians, we are called out for the express purpose of world evangelization to the glory of God.

Our Lord is thus building in us and through us His body on earth. He is building to perfection, and He is building to completion. He is building to a perfect oneness of God and man, and of man and man as united together in God. He is building also to the completion of His church body as to total membership.

He who builds thusly does not need any imperfect thing that finite man can give, raise up, or build for Him in human enterprise, as though man were able to add anything to the perfect One. Man himself is the one who is lacking wholeness. Nor can man find wholeness until he is willing to fit into God's great plan and purpose. The Lord's building of His church body is His plan and purpose. Why, then, do we Christians often get so all wrapped up in our building of physical church sanctuaries to the neglect of a concern for world missions, as necessary as these buildings are to house the local church body? Our Lord does not need to dwell in human-wrought projects because

The Lord Dwells in His Own Body
He Himself Is Building

with His own hands.

Here our Lord delights to dwell. Here we find the perfect One living in imperfect humanity. First we need to consider the perfection of the One doing the building and then consider the wonder of His building in and with us imperfect human beings, and what He is building toward.

The Lord Jesus Christ, being the God-man and One with the Father God and with the Spirit of God, is the only One who is both worthy and capable of being the Head of His one body. He alone of all people is both worthy and able as the "leader and commander" (Isa. 55:4) of the building enterprise of the ages because of all men He alone is preeminent (Col. 1:18).

He is preeminent since He is "the brightness of" the Father's "glory, and the express image of his person, and upholding all things by the word of his power, when he had by himself purged our sins, sat down on the right hand of the Majesty on high" (Heb. 1:3). Indeed, "in him dwelleth all the fulness of the Godhead bodily" (Col. 2:9), as well as "all the treasures of wisdom and knowledge" (v. 3).

He is preeminent since He is the risen Christ, the sovereign Lord not only over God's original creation of all things and beings, of which He is Creator, but the sovereign Lord as well over all of God's new creation: redeemed humanity, of whom He is the Saviour and Redeemer. Because of His resurrection triumph over sin, death, and all the powers of the underworld, His Father God has given to Him all power and all authority in heaven and earth. (See Matt. 28:18.) Furthermore, His Father has promised to yet give Him "the heathen for" His "inheritance, and the uttermost parts of the earth for" His "possession." (See Ps. 2:8.)

This temple body the Lord is building is unlike any other building the world knows anything about. The world cannot comprehend what the Lord is doing in and with His church. This is the deepest mystery, the most profound conundrum the world wonders after. Nothing like it has ever been. Here is God's greatest of all handiworks. Here is God's masterpiece. Here is God taking human beings—human lives marred and scarred by even the worst of sins and failures, lives that are misshapen misfits in even the world's society, lives ugly and in the eyes of the world of no value and of no promise—and reshaping, remolding, reworking us toward a perfection yet to come. Here is God taking people as different from each other, as high is from low, as poor is from rich, as despicable is from commendable, as east is from west, as north is from south, people from the most varied cultures and backgrounds in the world, and fusing us into a holy unity that is simply not of this world, a unity the perfecting of which is yet to be realized.

So what is our Lord building toward? We find the answer in Ephesians 1:10: "That in the dispensation of the fulness of times he might gather together in one all things in Christ, both which are in heaven, and which are on earth; even in him." The Lord's goal is the perfect, the complete realization of His Kingdom of which He spoke so often when here on earth. Already His Kingdom is here on earth in the hearts and lives of Christians who comprise His one church body worldwide. Each local church body Southern Baptists define as: "a church is the church in a given place and time."[1]

I'm thinking of a local church some one hundred miles from where I live that well exemplifies how God is at work today developing His masterpiece on an ever-enlarging scale of outreach. Binghamtown Baptist Church in the little city of Middlesboro, Kentucky, that has been pastored for years by Rev. W. B. Bingham, Sr., began about seven or eight years ago to experience a marvel of grace growth. Suddenly, this church began to stand tall in Christlike stature and reach out in Christlike compassion to the unreached people all about them. Brother Bingham's son, William Boyd, Jr., was voted in as assistant pastor to his father. Right away this able preacher and his dynamic evangelistic son began to expand their witness, and that of the church as a whole, both by television and visitation outreach. The crowds began to come. People began to respond to the gospel in greater numbers than ever before.

For years the church was attracting some two hundred people to its doors. But then the explosion of power came. Now their average attendance is around a thousand with thirteen to fifteen hundred often thronging their new church of unique architectural design that stands tall on its elevated vantage point, beckoning all Middlesboro and environs. Brother W. B., Sr., a personal friend of mine, tells me that during the past seven years well over seven hundred people have professed faith and been baptized into Binghamtown Baptist Church.

What is our Lord's purpose for His church on earth? For the church to so work in harmony with its Head that He through the members of His body can reach out to the unreached everywhere, to gather together in one all who will unite in one accord with Him.

The Lord's church body in the world today, each local congregation making up the whole, is His one, His only, agency of bringing to realization the sublime new order of His new creation already begun in reborn members of His church. How breathtaking indeed is this grand new order! "Behold, I make all things new" (Rev. 21:5), God has promised. Even the natural environment that environmentalists are so worried about as being in its present state of decline, God has promised to totally transform to be a part of the "new heavens and the new earth, God's glorious setting for his new creation, the perfect, the complete unity and order of which "Eye hath not seen, nor ear heard" (see 1 Cor. 2:9; also Isa. 64:4).

In his book: *World Mission and World Survival,* E. Luther Copeland gave remarkable insight into the new order of God's kingdom as being the goal of His church's global mission. "The kingdom of God," Dr. Copeland wrote "is the expression of God's sovereign control over history. This purposive control is not yet fully evident. There is an old order of things in which the powers of evil are at work. God has placed all things under the gracious sovereignty of Christ (1 Cor. 15:27). But the process of overcoming all the enemies of Christ, the powers of the old order, will continue until the end, and 'The last enemy to be defeated will be death' (1 Cor. 15:25-26, GNB). . . . The Kingdom is here with us in history, but it transcends history as the perfect norm which judges everything human as incomplete and imperfect."[2]

Dr. Copeland brings out that the world mission of the Lord's church body on earth "has to do with the good news of God's new order which has come into our world and our history in Jesus Christ." This our church's mission, he tells us, will continue until the end. Even unto the very end of history we are to testify of "God's far purpose" in His new order. This is the goal of our mission.[3] To this testimony we are bound by our Lord's strict orders in His Great Commission, even as we sing the grand old hymn, "Forward Through the Ages":

> Bound by God's far purpose
> In one living whole,
> Move we on together
> To the shining goal.[4]

Now our Lord is most concerned that we Christian members who comprise His one church body worldwide cooperate with Him and with one another in a partnership of unity in His great building plan because

The Lord's One Body
Remains as Yet Incomplete

The shining goal has not yet been reached. The goal is twofold since our Lord is building His body to spiritual maturity, and to evangelistic completion. Our Lord is building growthwise on a Christlike scale and missionwise on a world scale. Our Lord's goal for His church body in the one respect is "a perfect man," with His entire body thinking and functioning in perfect unity, as one individual in Christ, having attained to the "measure of the stature of the fulness of Christ" (Eph. 4:13). Christ's goal for His body worldwide in the other respect is "the whole body" as to completion of the entire membership that our Lord has in mind. This second aspect of the goal will have been reached only when "the whole body" is "fitly joined together and compacted by that which every joint supplieth, according to the effectual working in the measure of every part" (Eph. 4:16). This "whole body" cannot be whole memberwise until "every part," every member, has been added.

Since the first aspect of the goal can only be perfected through the completion of the second aspect, we must look first at exactly what the second aspect is. We must grasp what our Lord meant in His Great Commission when He commanded believers to evangelize every "nation." Did our Lord mean nations as we usually think of nations today, that is, as political units, or did He mean something more involved? The answer lies in the Greek word that Jesus used for "nations." The word is *ta ethne,* meaning "the peoples," or distinct ethnic units. In the book *The Unfinished Task,* Warren W. Webster spells out what Jesus meant when He commissioned us His followers to evangelize every nation:

"The task will not be finished until the gospel has been preached as a testimony to all nations. This does not mean simply all political nation states. Those borders have already been crossed. When Jesus commanded His followers to make disciples of all 'nations' he used the Greek word *ta ethne* from which we derive our word 'ethnic.' The word Jesus used for 'nations' can refer not only to nations as political units but to peoples, cultures, and tribes, each having a distinct ethnic, linguistic, or religious background. They are the 'nations' to be evangelized and discipled. If you want to know why our Lord did not return in the year A.D. 1000 or 1500 or 1900 or 1980, part of the answer is that the gospel had not yet been preached to all biblical nations. The end of the age awaits the completed proclamation to the ends of the earth."[5]

Now we begin to realize that far more nations are included in the unfinished task than we had been thinking. Within the some 223 political countries of the world today there are many biblical nations. To date all the continents have been reached, and all but eight of the countries. Yet *thousands* of nations remain unreached.

The Lord's one body is still incomplete because the task of world evangelization remains an unfinished task. The reason for this incompletion of members is the immaturity of the body. The Lord's body is not yet mature enough in oneness, in unity with our Head or with one another, to complete the job our Lord has assigned us. The fact that His assignment is an unfinished task is clear evidence of our spiritual lack.

Of course, we know that the "perfect man" is not going to be fully realized until the whole body on earth has been translated at our Lord's return for it. But how much progress toward that perfect goal must we realize before then?—enough to finish the unfinished task of world evangelization. And the more we Christians understand and contemplate the stupendous proportions of the unfinished task, the more we come to realize how much more maturity in unity it will require to accomplish the task.

In John 17:22-23, Jesus prayed to the Father God most urgently for our maturity in unity: "The glory which thou hast given me I have given to them, that they may be one even as we are one, I in them and thou in me, that they may become perfectly one, so that the world may know that thou hast sent me and hast loved them even as thou

hast loved me" (RSV). Reflecting upon our Lord's prayer
here, Winston Crawley in his book, *Global Mission*, points
out:

"The oneness described in the prayer of Jesus is spiritual oneness ('I in them and thou in me'). Southern Baptists have maintained that it does not prescribe
organizational unity. . . . However, sadly, Southern Baptists have been troubled from time to time by inner dis-
sension that has been a distraction from our mission and
has failed to reflect glory on the name of Christ. Furthermore, we have often failed to pursue biblical unity in
spirit with others who know, love, and serve the Lord
Jesus.

"Paul in Ephesians follows his emphasis on the mission
of the church (chapter 3) by urging the unity of the
church in the first half of chapter 4. Biblically, mission and
unity belong together."[6]

The *ekklesia* of our Lord is interpreted not only as the
called out but also as the called-together church body. We
are called out and called together for the same purpose.
We are called to be God's one united agent on earth for
the purpose of informing the whole world of God's great
plan of oneness in His Kingdom. How then can we be
content to strive against what our Lord Himself is working toward? And how can we be content to strive against
one another when our unity is so essential to our Lord's
purpose? We all need to consider just how interrelated,
interdependent, and thus inseparable is the Christlike
scale from the global scale on which our Lord is building
His church on earth.

Let us look more closely at this inseparable correlation.
How is Christian growth toward maturity on God's Christlike scale ever realized? Only as Christians worldwide
cooperate together in our Lord's world mission can we
make progress toward His dual goal for us of total evangel-

ization of the nations and mature Christlikeness. In Ephesians 3 Paul lays out for us God's guidelines in this direction.

Here Paul shows us how that the only way we can progress toward Christlikeness is to progress together toward Christ's global goal for us. Together we are called to "preach among the Gentiles (the 'nations') the unsearchable riches of Christ; and to make all men see what is the fellowship of the mystery" (v. 8-9) of God's great plan of bringing to oneness Himself and man, and man and man, which He purposed before the world's foundation. Now how can we make all people see this? Only as we let them see *our* Christian fellowship in growth toward Christlikeness. Then how can we grow in Christlikeness? Only as we grow together in His great mission cause of making all mankind see His purpose for them. "For this cause" our Lord is calling us to "bow" our "knees unto the Father of our Lord Jesus Christ" (v. 14). It is imperative that we look to God to supply our lack since we must realize that:

What the Lord's Body Lacks, He Alone
Who Lacks Nothing Is Able to Supply

For the fulfillment of "this cause" we must look to our Lord for three main ingredients that we are missing. We must look to Him upon our knees for our missing maturity, for our missing members, and for our missing power to find what we are missing. So how are we to so look to our Lord? As one "whole family" (v. 15).

"For this cause" we together are to pray that we be Spirit filled, "to be strengthened with might by his Spirit in the inner man" (v. 16). "For this cause" we together are to pray that by His Spirit, Jesus Christ will be incarnated in us, so He Himself can live again on earth in and through us as individual members of His one united body: "That Christ may dwell in your hearts by faith" (v. 17). "For this cause" each believer is to pray to be so "rooted and ground in love" that we are able "to comprehend" the fourfold dimensions of God's great love for the whole world and for every person in the whole world. How can we so "comprehend" God's great love? By each of us progressing together toward God's dual goal for us: each of us "with all saints" (see vv. 17-18).

How else can we as believers grow up together in Christ except as we grow outward in the vision of love and action of love to include all people everywhere in our mission plan? How else can we grasp the "breadth" of our Lord's love? How else can we grasp the "length" of His love than as we move ever onward with Him in His worldwide plan until the last biblical people group or "nation" has been reached with His gospel? How else can we grasp the "depth" of His love than as we are willing to descend together with Him into the foulest depths of earth's hell-holes after depraved, sunken sinners? How else can we grasp the "height" of His love than as we let Him use us to lift upward all sinners willing to yield to His magnetic love of Calvary, even let Him lift us all upward together to the heights of glory?

Do you really believe there is any other way that we of the Lord's body can "know the love of Christ, which passeth knowledge," and so "be filled with all the fulness of God"? (see v. 19).

Together we must look to our Lord upon our knees for our missing maturity since He as the one God-man is One with the Godhead in unity, and thus the only Man who is perfect and complete with the ability to bring humanity to the maturity of oneness.

In a certain midwestern state some years ago, a young child was missing. Quickly the news spread, and in no time flat, over three thousand people of the farming community had gathered to search for the missing child. It was discussed about how hard it would be ever to find the infant if they spread out and searched each one alone or even in pairs. Promptly they all decided to join hands. So hand in hand this wide cohesion of concerned neighbors began to move steadily across that wide-open prairie. It was not long until someone stumbled over the missing child. It is this kind of oneness that only our Lord can give us, and together we must look to Him for this oneness among ourselves.

Since we belong to the Godhead who is perfect in oneness, we cannot well live in oneness with our present immaturity.

Together we must look to our Lord upon our knees for our body and His body's missing members, since He is the only Authority who by His wisdom knows where the missing members are, and how to lead us to them. And since our Lord is complete as our Head, and we as His body remain incomplete, we cannot well live with our incompletion. Since our Lord is building to completion, how can we be content with incompletion? Since our Lord is building His church body on a global scale, how can we be content to build merely on a local scale? How can we ignore our body's missing members? Anyone who has had an arm or leg cut off knows how hard it is to live without the missing member. You can feel it; but it's not there. You want it, you very much need it; but it's not there. It's missing. Now we of the Lord's body must look to our Lord in prayer to arouse in us a sense of that which is missing until we cry aloud for it, until we have a fever of concern to go and find our missing members. Let us pray until we hear a voice, as Kipling wrote:

> Something hidden. Go and find it. Go
> and look behind the Ranges—
> Something lost behind the Ranges.
> Lost and waiting for you. Go![7]

Together upon our knees we must look to our Lord for our missing power to grow to the mature unity we need to find our missing members. We must look to Him for our missing power to finish our task. We must look to Him for our missing strength. For our missing energy. Our missing dynamic ability. In ourselves we are weak; we are totally unable to find and win those among the world's hidden peoples who will complete that which is missing from our Lord's one body. Our Lord reminds us, "Without me ye can do nothing" (John 15:5). We must look to Him who is all-sufficient and the Source of all power and ability. We must look to Him who is the sole Administrator of this power to usward. We must look to Him, believing "what is the exceeding greatness of his power to us-ward who believe, according to the working of his mighty power" (Eph. 1:19). We must look to Him who "is able to do exceeding abundantly above all that we ask or think, according to the power that worketh in us," that "unto him [might] be glory in the church by Christ Jesus throughout all ages, world without end. Amen" (Eph. 3:20-21). (See also Col. 1:29; 2:19.)

Now not only must we look to Him who alone lacks nothing to supply our missing oneness, our missing members, and our missing power, but if we expect an answer, we must look to Him in the same spirit that the one hundred and twenty men and women looked to Him before Pentecost came: in one accord. We must be in one accord of submission, in one accord of waiting, and in one accord of expectancy. (See Acts 1:14 *ff.*) Not long ago our local church spent ten weeks in concentrated study of the past spiritual awakenings God has given us, especially those in America. We found that in each instance before the fire fell, these same conditions prevailed, and most assuredly, the Heavenly Fire we must have to complete the unfinished task of world evangelization.

In our local church work we must avoid the chronic condition that someone has described as "ingrown eyeballs"—eyes focused solely upon ourselves and our own doings, eyes that do not see beyond. We must realize that whatever we attempt to give, work out, or build up in our own plans and power does not count with God. We must realize that our Lord is engaged in His own building plan, and that what counts with Him is for us to let Him use us in His great global plan. Furthermore, in our self-obsession we sense a sore vacuum. If we would turn to ask our Lord: "What does our church lack?" we might very well hear Him give answer by way of the following account related by Marilyn Laszlo who is a missionary with Wycliffe Bible Translators:

> For the past thirteen years I have been working in Haunna, a little village which is 500 miles up the Sepik River in the heart of the jungle of Papua New Guinea, an island just north of Australia. . . .
> As we translated and taught the people to read and write their own language, we became burdened for all of the unreached tribes around us. Hauna was becoming a shining light throughout the area as people started to hear about our work. One day a canoe loaded with fifteen people came for medical help. They spoke another tribal language and came into our house with the smell of their rotting sores and other diseases. I told them in the trade language, Pidgin English, that they must stay in our village at least a week so I could give them a penicillin series for their sores.
> While they stayed with us they watched what was going on. They saw 200 people coming to school to learn to read and write their own language. They saw us write God's talk in the people's language and listened to the Sepik Iwam pastors preach the Word of God in their own language.
> When it was time for them to go home, the leader asked, "Do you think you could come to my village and put down our talk so that we might know about God too?"

I had to shake my head and say, "I'm not finished here yet. I have several more years of work in this place." I could tell he was very disappointed, and I promised that someday I would at least come to visit his village.

Several weeks later we organized a party to find his village. When we got there, the leader was thrilled to see us. He called everybody to come and see the two white misses. As we were walking through the village I noticed in the center a new building, very different from their regular houses. I asked, "What is that building there in the center of the village?"

He said, "Oh, that is God's house—that's our church."

"Your church? Do you have a mission here?"

Oh, no, we have never had a mission here."

"Well, do you have a pastor here—you know, someone that comes to preach God's Word?"

"Oh, no, we've never had a pastor here."

"Well, is there someone here in the village that can read and write Pidgin English who holds services in your church?"

"Oh, no! There is no one here that can read or write. And we have no books."

I looked at him and said, "Then what is that building for?"

He said, "Well, we saw the little church in your village and our people decided to build a church too. Now we're waiting for someone to come and tell us about God in our own talk."

I turned and started crying. I have never seen that kind of faith. Out in the middle of the jungle stands that little church, and today they are still waiting—waiting for someone to come and tell them in their own language about Jesus. There are thousands of groups just like them, waiting to hear the Word of God in their own language. They are waiting for you.[8]

In answer to our question: "What does our church lack?" we might very well hear Jesus say, "The only way I can fulfill your church lack is for you to let Me use you to meet the church lack of people groups like this." Here

are people with a church building filled with much unconverted, undeveloped humanity, waiting for a preacher to
bring them the gospel. All they have is a building made
with human hands. What they need to know is how they
can receive Christ, who greatly desires to dwell in them
and make them a part of His great building plan, since
"The God who made the world . . . does not dwell in
temples made with hands" (Acts 17:24-25, NASB). What
they need to learn—and what we need to remember, so
we can go and tell them—is: "There is one body" (Eph.
4:4) where the true God dwells, one temple body that He
is building to a perfect oneness and to a complete whole
with His own spiritual hands; but the only tangible hands
which He has to complete His church body on earth is our
hands, and their hands, without which the Lord's one
body is as yet incomplete.

(Now all the Athenians and the strangers visiting there used to spend their time in nothing other than telling or hearing something new) (Acts 17:21, NASB). I was a stranger, and ye took me in . . . I was a stranger, and ye took me not in (Matt. 25:35-43).

11
Countless Strangers to the Lord's One Body

Paul included in his compassionate witness not only Athenians but likewise the strangers visiting among them. So would our Lord have us Christians to include in our concerned outreach the many strangers both in our midst and far away. As we have seen in chapter 10, our Lord has commissioned us to all the nations. This encompasses both the reached and the unreached people groups of the world. Both at home and abroad, these two groups are to be found. Both at home and abroad, unreached people groups are to be found. Throughout this book I am stressing an equal concerned outreach to both the reached and the unreached peoples of our world. Yet since the unreached of our Lord's Great Commission have been so much more neglected than the reached, I am urging that we join those already much concerned in our denomination, and in other true Christian denominations and groups, in an all-out effort to find and reach them with the gospel.

These unreached at home and abroad are strangers to the Lord's one body on earth. We often hear them referred to also as "hidden-people" groups or "frontier" groups. These "hidden" peoples are strangers to us of the church because they are "hidden from our view and the conventional outreach of existing churches and mission agencies. 'Frontier' missions is thus a critical complement to 'regular' missions if new beachheads for the gospel are to be established within still untouched cultural groups."[1]

How then shall we define an unreached or "hidden" people? According to Edward R. Dayton, founder of World Vision's Missions Advanced Research and Communications Center (MARC), an *"unreached people is a group that is less than 20 percent practicing Christian.* Why was the figure 20 percent chosen as a dividing line between unreached and reached peoples? . . . By the time 10-20 percent of a group accepts a new idea, enough momentum may well have been built up so that subsequent increases of acceptance will be rapid."[2]

A more recent definition, however, is that an unreached people is a people group "among which there is no indigenous community of believing Christians with adequate numbers and resources to evangelize this people group without outside (cross-cultural) assistance."[3]

Again, an unreached or "hidden" people has been defined by Dayton, Winter, and others as a people that have not been penetrated by the gospel, and that have no viable, evangelizing, indigenous church planted within them as a group.[4] "By viable we understand a church that has within itself the capacity to spread the good news through the rest of this 'sociological grouping who have a common affinity for one another.' "[5]

There may even be a church in their geographical area, but if it doesn't belong to their particular culture, the people group is still classified as unreached and hidden. In their area there may even be a handful of Christians who worship in churches of another cultural tradition, and there may even be a few missionaries in their area. But if there is no indigenous church for their own culture, the people group is still hidden from the outreach of the true church. These peoples remain strangers to the Lord's one body on earth. Because our Lord is very much concerned about these hidden peoples, and because (according to Ralph Winter) less than 10 percent of the world's missionaries and only 5 percent of mission money are now being focused on these 17,000 groups,[6] we may be quite sure that our Lord desires that no one who belongs to Him overlook or ignore them in any wise. If you will get your concordance and run down the words *stranger* and *strangers* throughout the Bible, I am sure that you will agree that

Our Lord Is Calling Us to Love
These Strangers Among Us and Far from Us

The Bible has much to say concerning the strangers in our world. God includes them in His boundless love, and He commands us Christians to love them. In Deuteronomy 10:19 we are commanded: "Love ye therefore the stranger: for ye were strangers in the land of Egypt." Our Lord reminds us that at one time we were, each of us, a stranger. "Wherefore remember . . . that at that time ye were without Christ, being aliens from the commonwealth of Israel, and strangers from the covenants of promise, having no hope, and without God in the world" (Eph. 2:11-12). We therefore are commanded to exercise heartfelt compassion toward all strangers to the church everywhere who are "without Christ," "having no hope, and without God in the world." God would have us of His true church body to inform these strangers that He certainly wants them, "aliens" though they are, to accept His Son and join His great Kingdom order and cause. He wants them to know that He wants them in on His "covenant of promise." He wants them to understand that His Kingdom is not exclusive unless they exclude themselves by refusal of His Son. In Ezekiel 47:22 God says, "The strangers that sojourn among you . . . they shall have inheritance with you among the tribes of Israel." Oh, how wonderful that our God shuts no one out! And our God has made it our job to let the strangers know they are not shut out.

God commands us to show the stranger not only justice but also mercy and kindness. He warns of judgment upon all who "turn aside the stranger from his right" (see Mal. 3:5).

Now God lets us know that if we are to love the stranger, this surely means that we provide for his needs. In Leviticus the Lord instructs us: "When ye reap the harvest of your land . . . thou shalt leave" (a portion of grain, grapes, etc.) "for the poor and stranger" (19:9-10).

Now if we of the Lord's body are to provide for the needs of those who are strangers to us, we must learn what their needs are. The only way we can reach them and win them to our Lord is through meeting their needs. Edward R. Dayton in an article entitled "To Reach the Unreached" specified how we should go about reaching them through their need. "How do we reach them?" Dayton asked:

> By trying to know them as God knows them.
> By attempting to meet their need as they see it.
> By communicating the saving power of Jesus Christ in their language and in their cultural understanding and in terms of where they are.
> In order to communicate to people we have to begin where they perceive their need. . . . Understanding a people through their need is basic to the strategy . . . that is useful anywhere in the world.[7]

We have to learn what the lost are searching for, what their hearts are longing for. In disaster-striken areas of the world, for example, we know exactly what their longing is. It is for food, medical attention, and so forth. And it is only through meeting these emergency physical needs that we can gain their confidence, whereby we can then find what their basic heart longing is, and so reach them for Christ. At a Foreign Missions Week at Ridgecrest, we heard numerous testimonies to the amazing results this strategic approach is bringing in many areas. Southern Baptists move into a needy area, promptly meeting the utter starvation and disease of the people, and find them immediately asking, "When can you Baptists begin preaching here, and begin building churches here?" Without the famine, the hunger, the bodily affliction, and our administering to them in their extremity, we might very well never have found access first to their confidence and then to their longing for God.

We do well to note that Paul in Athens was not only concerned with the longing of the Athenians but likewise with that of the strangers visiting there. He found such to be the same for both. Both were searching for the latest fad. Actually, both were restless for the same thing—the same thing that souls are restless for everywhere on earth today. "Oh, Lord, our souls are restless," Augustine acknowledged long ago, "till they rest in Thee."

But before we can know and provide for the need of these strangers to our Lord's body, we must know that

Our Lord Is Calling Us to Learn Who and Where These Strangers Are

They are in the world's people groups. They are both the "stranger that is within thy gates" (Ex. 20:10) and the strangers scattered throughout the limits of the regions beyond. Both are hidden or separated from the Lord's church body by definite boundary lines or barriers. These barriers may be barriers of geography, language, culture, religion, economy, and so forth, or a combination of these.

My research disclosed that these strangers fall largely within one or more of the following classifications:

Strangers Hidden Among the Nations Within the World's Countries

Already in chapter 10 we have understood the meaning of biblical "nations." Here is an example. Prior to British colonization of that part of Africa they termed British East Africa, there were at least twenty-four different nations living in that territory. These same twenty-four different nations are living there today within the country of Kenya. So it is in countries all over the world. We have yet to reach so many of the nations within the countries. Our job will not be done until we reach all these strangers within all these nations within all the countries containing distinct tribes or cultures. God has promised, "I will gather all nations and tongues; and they shall come, and see my glory" (Isa. 66:18).

Now, how is our Lord going to gather these strangers hidden among all nations and tongues? Only as we let Him use us to find who and where they are. So many yet remain hidden from the eyes of the church and thus hidden from the light of the gospel of saving grace.

Strangers Hidden Among the World's Many Languages and Dialects

Not only is our Lord depending upon us of His body to find the many strangers among the many nations, but likewise among the many tongues of the world.

Basic to reaching the many within the many tongues is Bible translation. C. Peter Wagner, in his book *On the Crest of the Wave: Becoming a World Christian,* brought an update on Bible translation. He wrote:

> Bible translation has made tremendous progress. There

is some Scripture in over 1,763 languages, covering 97 percent of the world's population. But the remaining challenge is twofold. First, the Scriptures need to be translated into the remaining 3,000 languages and dialects. The notion that the dialects will disappear with the modernization of the world is a myth. In many parts of the world minority dialects are becoming more, not less, popular.

The second aspect of the challenge is to revise current translations. Bible translation technology is so advanced that we now recognize that many translations are embarrassingly inaccurate and obsolete. To help meet this challenge, the Fuller School of World Mission has recently teamed with Wycliffe Bible Translators in the first graduate program in Bible translation leading to a Ph.D. Dan Shaw of Papua, New Guinea is directing the program.[8]

Now let us see how the remaining language groups of unreached peoples look when broken down into the different regions of the world. Sam Wilson and Gordon Aeschliman of MARC ministry, referred to earlier, in a book called *The Hidden Half: Discovering the World of Unreached Peoples,* offered this table:

REGIONS OF THE WORLD
UNREACHED PEOPLES AS LANGUAGE GROUPS

REGION	TOTAL LANGUAGES	NUMBER OF UNREACHED PEOPLES*
Africa	1883	1034
East Asia	193	62
Europe	169	10
Latin America	1538	200
Northern America	250	11
Oceania	1253	629
South Asia	1596	976
USSR	128	59

* A total of 2,981 unreached peoples of different languages. The *total* number of unreached people groups is greater than this because many unreached peoples share languages.[9]

The previous table should give us considerable insight.

Strangers Hidden Among the World's False Religions

While there are many false religions in the world today, I will mention only the five containing the largest blocks of unreached peoples. These are Islam, Hinduism, Buddhism, tribalism, and Chinese traditionalism.

The largest and most awesome of these, since it is the fastest growing, is Islam. Islam, second only to Christianity in its spread over our world at this hour, is indeed growing by leaps and bounds. Islam is on the upsurge far and wide over the earth, appealing to masses in many different cultures, languages, and life-styles. There are major concentrations of fanatical devotees across Europe and Asia all the way to, and including, Mainland China. Many other parts of the world as well are fast falling under its spell. In England, Muslim mosques are going up everywhere. Even in America, Islam is one of our most forbidding dangers to the spread of the gospel of Christ. Worldwide, Islam claims somewhere between 800 and 850 million followers. This means that one out of every five persons on earth is a Muslim!

Second to Islam comes Hinduism. Not as threatening to all the world as Islam since its major concentration of adherents is found in India, but it is, nevertheless, a net for souls. Its multitude of deities and spirits vie for multitudes of souls. It is locking many into the coils of its karma or fate. Hinduism lays claim to between 600 and 650 million people now.

Third in number of devotees is Buddhism. Offering its unending cycle of reincarnation and suffering, Buddhism is swallowing many around the world, including a growing number in our own USA. Altogether Buddhism claims something around 300 million souls.

Fourth in size come the tribal groups. While numerous tribes have taken on a veneer of Hinduism, Buddhism, and Islam, the great majority remain animists, captive to their various evil spirits. It is reported that as many as five thousand distinct tribes still do not have any church among them.[10] Tribalism claims between 100 and 200 million people.

Fifth in number of devotees is Chinese Traditionalism with something like 200 million souls led its way.

In his chart entitled "Unreached Peoples of the World 1985" Ralph Winter showed among Muslims, Hindus, Buddhists, and Tribals alone 1,300 unreached peoples groups.[11]

Strangers Hidden Among the World's Big and Fast-Growing Cities

From the days of Jesus until around 1800, only 3 percent of the world lived in cities. Now experts who study the population explosion estimate that by the year 2000 half of the people on earth will be living in urban areas.

It is estimated that every month the world grows by two new "Chicagos." It is believed that by the year 2000 there will be some twenty-nine cities larger than New York City now is. This growth in city population is because the world's population is shifting significantly. In Africa alone within the past twenty years, seventy-five million people have left their rural areas for the cities.

What must be the response of the Lord's body to this vast influx of strangers into the very midst of our cities worldwide? Missionaries call for 25,000 new urban congregations to reach the seventy-five million Africans who have moved to the cities. This challenge is ringing forth by concerned Christians regarding the rapidly increasing need in cities everywhere.

As world cities swell in size, so swells the festering sore.

Rising unemployment and dwindling food supplies will continue to result in dire poverty. That in turn will spread disease, disillusionment, and dispair. Oh, church body of the living Lord, stand forth! You are needed now. Strangers are knocking at your doors.

Strangers Hidden Among the World's Uprooted Wanderers

Long ago, even in Daniel's day, God through His prophet foretold of the world's many refugees in the last days. Daniel 12:4 declares that at the time of the end "many shall run to and fro."

Many of the millions pouring into the cities are not going to remain in the same city. Many are on a lifetime search for settlement, for stability, for meaning to life itself.

Many, even practically all, of these uprooted wanderers have been forced to leave their homes on very short and unexpected notice. Only the smaller number have been uprooted by natural disaster. The majority have been uprooted by political and economic turmoil of governments and change of governments and conditions in their native countries that have left them with no way to provide a living where they were.

Millions, and ever-growing millions, around the world are on the unending move. Millions continue to pour into the USA. They are literally knocking upon our American church doors. One of the ripest mission fields today is in our midst! Would our Lord have us become acquainted with and seek to give hope and solution to these many uprooted ones so desperately groping for that "something new" that the strangers in Athens were searching for? Many of the refugees have little idea what that "something new" that will give them life purpose really is. But we of our Lord's body know. Shall we tell them? What are we waiting for?

Strangers Hidden Among the World's Poor and Very Poor

As the cities grow and the masses wander, dire poverty proliferates alarmingly. Not only those on the move, but many remaining where they are are victims of growing physical need. What are the growing results of world poverty? Wilson and Aeschliman tell us, "The poorest third of the world's countries have average infant mortality rates of 140 deaths per 1,000 live births. Those who survive infancy can only expect to live to be forty-seven; only 28 percent of the men and 9 percent of the women will ever learn to read. These countries have gross national products (GNP) averaging $320 per person per year."[12]

Missionaries remind us middle-class Americans that many on the missions fields consider us rich people. Compared to them in their need we are rich! Shall we share with them? In Leviticus 19:10 our Lord commands us not to lavish all our rich harvest upon ourselves alone. Our Lord says "thou shalt leave them (portions of grapes and grain) for the poor and stranger: I am the Lord your God."

How much more are we to share the true riches? Certainly, our Lord would have us recognize the same of ourselves as He recognized of Himself, "The Spirit of the Lord is upon me, because he hath anointed me to preach the gospel to the poor" (See Luke 4:18 *ff.*; Isa. 61:1 *ff.*)

Strangers Hidden Among the World's Rich and Very Rich

The rich—and especially the very rich of this world—while not nearly so numerous as the world's poor and very poor are likewise a much-neglected segment of society. Behind the barricade of wealth wait many strangers to the

Lord's gospel and to the Lord's one body on earth. And no more would our Lord have us neglect them than He would have us neglect the poor. Our Lord loves all alike.

It is true that a good number of wealthy people have barricaded—and continue to barricade—themselves from Christians and from the gospel. Many do not want to be bothered. Certain evangelicals have reported iron doors, and often guarded doors, barring their access to the rich in Gibraltar, for example. These Christians request our prayers for access to these and other "needy" rich people. Many rich persons mistake our motive. So many simply refuse to believe that the Lord's love includes them. Many others, who also have not been reached, actually long secretly for someone to come and share with them the news of the gospel of saving grace.

An overseas missionary at home on furlough in the USA stood looking wistfully out the window of a large but dwindling city church. As he watched bustling activities across the street, he was listening more attentively than he appeared to the heartbroken lament of the church secretary, a lifelong member of the church. She kept pouring out to him the sad refrain of so many people leaving her beloved church in recent years. Some had been promoted to glory. Others had moved to distant locations. Most of the ones leaving had moved to outlying suburban areas where they had joined churches near their new homes.

"What is going to happen to us here?" the missionary heard her ask, as out of the corner of his eye he observed tiny tears glistening in her eyelashes. "Already the upper five stories of our educational building are unused. Three fourths of our sanctuary pews are unfilled even at our Sunday morning worship hour. Only a handful show up for Sunday night and Wednesday night services."

"That is heartrending all right," agreed the foreign missionary, watching men working like ants just across from them.

"What on earth are we going to do? Continue to wilt until we die on the stem?"

"I certainly do not believe that needs to happen."

"Well then, what miracle do you propose?"

"A miracle God waits able and ready to perform, my dear."

"A miracle? In truth?"

The missionary turned to confront his friend of long acquaintance. "Just look across the street there," he said, jerking his thumb in that direction.

"Yes; oh, yes, that's another one of those many housing developments we see going up everywhere all over town anymore."

"And this one you can almost brush with your elbow every time you swivel in your desk chair."

"Yes, I can't hear myself think for all the noise."

"It's quieter Sunday mornings when you worship?"

"Unless they're working then too! It won't be much quieter when all the people move in, either."

"But there, I believe Jesus would tell you, is your answer," the missionary returned, spinning back around to watch the construction in process.

"The answer? For *us*?"

"For who else anymore than for you people?"

"Yes, of course; but I—I'm afraid some of our members would object. Some of these people we might reach; but I fear that too many of our members would find most of these people hardly in our class."

"But they're the same kind of people Jesus welcomed in His day: the same classes that flocked out to follow our Lord when they saw His open arms inviting them. Why don't you people invite them?"

"Oh, but our members *are* missionary minded. They

love to watch slides of you missionaries cuddling dirty, hungry, little foreign children. They give liberally to both home and foreign missions."

"But what about the blue-collar strangers to our Lord's local church right here in your front door? Will *you* go and win *them?*"

This situation is quite significant because it is not isolated. So many of our homeland churches are slowly but surely dying with God's clear answer to their dilemma right across from them.

Strangers Hidden Among the World's Wild Crowd

The world's wild crowd takes in not only certain of the idle rich who, finding time hanging heavy on their hands, fall into one endless round of licentious pursuits, but likewise many not so rich. While we Christians are warned of God not to run "with them to the same excess of riot" (1 Pet. 4:4; see also vv. 1-3), we are not to scorn them either. In truth, many of the most noteworthy Christians of the past and present were once given to this life-style. Some of us all too quickly forget the depths of sin our merciful Lord has claimed us from when we consider today's wild crowd beyond our compassion.

We must also consider just how much of the Bible is devoted to our merciful Lord's concern for all prodigal sons and prodigal daughters still on the self-indulgent road to hell. We ought to think about how many such have yielded to the amazing grace of God as proclaimed to them by concerned soul-winners. The Bible is filled with reports of their marvelous conversions, as are many accounts written since the Bible. Jesus Himself warned the hypocrites that the publicans and harlots would go into the kingdom of God before them. (See Matt. 21:31-32.)

I thank and praise God, then, for the soul-winners who seek and win as many "wild things" as they can.

Strangers Hidden Among the World's Captives

All of the world's wild crowd are captives of sin and of Satan, but many of this group have gone so far in reckless living that they have fallen captive to man as well. Many others of them have ventured into crime and thus fallen captive to the governments of society.

Among those who have fallen captive to their fellow-men are many nightclub performers and prostitutes of both sexes. These sad human beings with immortal souls are victims of violence, threats of worse violence, intolerable abuse and oppression, and isolation from those concerned enough to reach out a helping hand or offer them a word of Scripture. Strangers to us of our Lord's body they are in every sense of the word. And such captives of sin, Satan, and men are to be found in every country and in every culture, especially among dense and poor populations. Many such are so scared for their lives that few of them ever find deliverance, because soul-winners rarely break through the barriers their captors have placed around them. But our Lord loves them none the less, nor is His command to seek and win them less binding upon us.

Then there are the many criminals who, because of their falling into crime, are captives of society. They too are truly objects of our Lord's compassion. In spite of their guilt our Lord extends to them His offer of forgiveness. Thank God for Prison Fellowship organized and directed by Charles Colson, former Nixon aide, who by his winning many such prisoners to Christ (as well as by his plans and procedures to win many more) gives the world every evidence of his own new birth.

There is no better way for believers to give evidence of their new birth than by extending the gospel of saving grace to the world's captives of every kind.

Strangers Hidden Among the World's Students

I am burdened constantly that so few of our world's students are being reached and won with the gospel. The world's students for the most part are the world's youth. Practically every form of drugs, vice, false ideology and false religion known to humanity now has access to students. One concept that seldom has access to them is the gospel of Jesus Christ.

Drug peddlers now have ready access to many students on all levels of learning. Instructors of false systems of thought that lead to fatal life-styles likewise have, all too often, ready access to many students on all levels of learning. The secular humanists in our own USA, for example, have declared their avowed purpose to use their pulpits to reach and indoctrinate the youth of our nation at all levels of learning from kindergarten to college and university level. Meanwhile, we of our Lord's body, far too many of us, stand idly by, wringing our hands and declaring that there is absolutely nothing we can do to correct the imbalance of false and true teaching now having access to our students and to so many of the world's students. We need to remember that as go the youth, so goes the nation and all nations.

The fact that wherever in this world, for example, in Korea, evangelists and other Christian witnesses are permitted access to centers of learning, the Holy Spirit of God is using such witness to win many youth to the Savior. This is irrefutable proof that God's Spirit no more considers the world's centers of learning off limits to a presentation of the gospel than He does the haunts of the wild crowd, or the living quarters of the refugees, or the locales of any of the other unreached strangers to the Lord's body today.

Now while the above classifications may very well not

exhaust the divisions in which the world's unreached peoples are hidden in today's world, they do seem to form the principal barriers behind which the unreached are hidden.

Realizing our Lord is extremely concerned that His one church body remains incomplete as to total members, we of that body must listen closely to hear our Lord's voice, because according to God's Word

Our Lord Is Calling Us to Search Out from Among These Strangers Builders

who will serve as both building blocks and builders for His completion of His great building plan of the ages: His one church body. As these hidden peoples groups continue to be evangelized, more and more persons among them will believe on the Savior and so become incorporated into our Lord's great plan and purpose. Many will fall in beside of us as most useful co-laborers with our Lord and with us. Our Lord's great building work is not going to be complete without them.

We do well to recall that when God commanded His servant David to gather together both building material and builders for His magnificent Temple that David's son Solomon was to build, "David commanded to gather together the strangers that were in the land of Israel" to help build the house of the Lord God (1 Chron. 22:2). Then when it came Solomon's time to build, he had a census taken to determine the total number of these strangers and found them to be 153,600 altogether. Of these Solomon assigned 70,000 to labor as carriers and 80,000 to labor as stonecutters in the hills, and the remaining 3,600 strangers to serve as foremen over the others. (See 2 Chron. 2:17-18.)

Fellow members of the Lord's body worldwide, we do well to take serious note that this building plan of our

Lord God, as in the days of David and Solomon, has not changed. God still determines to use us who are already building blocks and laborers to search out worldwide strangers to His body to labor beside us to the completion of His great plan of the ages.

So, it is of the utmost importance that we go to every length to find, to love, and to win many strangers from among the earth's peoples, because our Lord Himself reminds us that

To Ignore These Strangers
Is to Ignore Our Lord

In His foretelling of that great day of judgment when He comes in His glory, our Lord Jesus warned us all of the basis on which He will divide the sheep from the goats (Matt. 25:31-46). Among other things, He declares that we shall be declared sheep if He can say concerning our treatment of our fellowmen, "Come, ye blessed of my Father, inherit the kingdom prepared for you from the foundation of the world: For . . . I was a stranger, and ye took me in" (vv. 34-35). But then, among other things, He likewise declared that we shall be declared goats if He has to say concerning our treatment of our fellowmen, "Depart from me, ye cursed, into everlasting fire, prepared for the devil and his angels: For . . . I was a stranger, and ye took me not in" (vv. 41-43). So, then, brothers and sisters, how shall we of our Lord's body today behave in our treatment of these strangers to our Lord's body? Shall we behave as sheep or as goats?

Our Lord reminds us that our attitude toward these strangers as to our acceptance or our rejection of them is our precise attitude toward our Lord Himself. We would do well to consider whether we are treating Jesus as the prophet Jeremiah saw Him treated and wondered at such treatment: "O the hope of Israel, the saviour thereof in time of trouble, why shouldst thou be as a stranger in the land . . . . as a mighty man that cannot save?" (14:8-9).

Our Lord is deeply concerned that we who are His respond with an all-out compassionate witness to the many strangers to His church body worldwide at this strategic hour. As were the strangers in Athens to whom Paul witnessed, these many strangers today are very hungry for "some new thing" to fill the pitiful emptiness they sense inside them.

This soul hunger I encountered on every hand on my recent preaching mission to Chile. I was one of the members of a Partnership Evangelism team sent by the Southern Baptist Foreign Mission Board to preach in a simultaneous crusade of thirty-three South Chilean churches and missions. Everywhere I witnessed, in the hotels, shops, streets, and homes, as well as in the church where I preached, I found this hunger for the gospel. Everyone to whom I witnessed wanted to hear more. Government and military officials of high rank, as well as the men under them, asked for details concerning God's plan of salvation.

The waitress serving us in our hotel in Santiago kept wanting to hear more. The bellboy who carried our luggage in our hotel in Valdivia desired to hear more. The many thronging the streets in both cities were eager to receive and read at once the gospel booklets we handed them. I found no one indifferent to our message. I saw no gospel literature discarded anywhere.

When we witnessed to the mayor of Valdivia, to the military governor, and the chief of the government police over the Austral District (which takes in much of South Chile), we were graciously received. Each one was pleased to receive the Bible, the Gospel booklet, and the personal testimony we gave. When I told the chief of police that the literature I was giving him answered the question people all over the world are asking, that is, "How can I find peace with God?" the chief's eyes brightened. When I told him how I myself found this peace, he listened more intently. When I said that God gave me full assurance of this peace with Him when I confessed myself a lost sinner and trusted Christ's shed blood to cancel my sin penalty, the chief replied, "I too desire this peace with God that people all over the world are searching for. I will be looking forward to learning more about it very soon from this gospel literature."

When we witnessed in a military regiment, both the colonel and the captain who received us kept asking for more information concerning how to be saved. Then the colonel invited some of us to preach a message to the soldiers. More and more soldiers kept pouring into the building to hear the gospel. Each soldier leaned forward in his chair, listening in rapt attention. After the sermon, hands were raised everywhere requesting prayer.

Then when I preached for one week in the little church, the building was often jammed with people listening hungrily. Most of the nonmembers attending were not used to hearing an invitation to come forward on public profession of faith in Jesus. They hesitated, and yet they came. In answer to much prayer, God moved upon them, and they came. In increasing numbers they publicly came to Jesus. I praise God for everyone who came.

Among those who came to Jesus was a young adult named Susana. She had had a brother to commit suicide, and she was hurting inside and hungry for the love of God. When we came to her aunt's home to tell her of God's love, Susana went upstairs to get a Bible. When she came back down, she followed in her aunt's Bible every word I spoke. Yet Susana said she doubted that God really loved her. Besides her doubting, she feared what her immediate family would say should she publicly accept Jesus Christ.

But three days later, Susana made her decision. And she made it publicly. When she heard me challenge all to take up the cross, forsaking all for the Christ who took up His cross for us, Susana came forward. The joy radiating from her face told the story. Susana had proven God's love for her.

We members of this Partnership Evangelism team praise God for the hungry response to the gospel in South Chile. Yet we cannot forget the faces of the masses flooding the streets who have not been reached with the gospel. The number and the need of the unreached strangers to the Lord's church body is overwhelming. The empty look in the eyes of the unreached stranger is a look of intense soul hunger.

12
Jesus' One Challenge
to the Members of His Body

For the first time since the beginning of his missionary journeys, Paul arrived in Athens to find himself absolutely alone. Silas and Timothy were still in Berea. Surrounded by idols and the populace whose lives centered around idols, Paul must have sensed an overwhelming exasperation. As *The Living Bible* renders Acts 17:16: "He was deeply troubled by all the idols he saw everywhere throughout the city." Phillips translates it: "His soul was exasperated at the sight." Here he was in the middle of an overwhelming need, and all alone to meet it. For a while, Paul must have recoiled before the seemingly impossible. Paul must have felt as the disciples did when the 5,000 had come out to hear Jesus, and the day was nearing night. The many had to be fed, but they had only five loaves and two fish. The difficulty seemed insuperable.

Paul, however, did not conclude, as did the disciples, that the only solution was to send the many away empty, their need unfulfilled. Though his spirit was in deep distress, exasperated at the sight, as Phillips puts it further, "He felt compelled to discuss the matter" both with the Jews and with the pagans in the synagogue, as well as with all the passers-by in the public marketplace. No doubt he who challenged Paul was the Spirit of the same Jesus who challenged the disciples in the face of the seemingly impossible: "You feed them!"

We Christians today feel overwhelmed by what seems far more impossible than either the disciples' 5,000 needing physical food or Paul's city full of idol worshipers needing the one true gospel. We today are confronted by a world of lost and famished humanity, not only numbering into the billions, but rapidly increasing in number at an alarming rate. In the teeth of a task that seems quite beyond us, we feel our smallness, our weakness, our futility.

Nontheless,

In Spite of the Ever-Mushrooming Many, Still Jesus Challenges Us: "You Feed Them!"

In the apostolic era there were perhaps some 275 million people on earth. When challenged by their Lord, "You are to go into all the world and preach the Good News to everyone, everywhere" (Mark 16:15, TLB), the apostles knew that they truly had a task before them. But by the time of William Carey, when the church again began to awaken to hear Jesus' challenge to include the whole world in its evangelistic plans, the world population had grown to about 900 million. The number of people to be fed had tripled. Not only had the gap widened from the first century to near the nineteenth, but while the church had slumbered during this long period, literally millions had slipped out into a Christless eternity. After the passing of the first-century apostles, the evangelistic fervor of Pentecost began to wane. Up until the time of Carey, most Christians took Jesus' worldwide challenge lightly.

Then came Carey with his famous challenge to his fellow Christians. In 1793 the era of modern missions began. Much of the church awakened to see its task as not only unfinished but mushrooming to the ends of the earth. But, even though more and more churches began to send out more and more volunteer ambassadors to the unreached masses, by the middle of the nineteenth century the world population had swollen to more than 1 billion people. By the time the 1930s had been reached, the number of souls on earth had blown up already to the 2 billion extent. Then by 1960, our world inhabitants had grown in number to around 3 billion. By 1975 they had become 4 billion. Now, as of 1988, the 5 billion mark has been reached.

As we head toward the 1990s, we stand aghast at our task's enormity. Though on the part of Southern Baptists and several other evangelicals our missions vision is ever broadening, and our missions plans and procedures are ever accelerating, we realize that we are still far behind in the numbers race. Each day the people of our world, most of whom are as yet unfed with the Bread of life, grow in number by more than 200,000 persons. That's around 70 million per year. Already we have passed the 5 billion mark in world population. Population experts project that by the year AD 2000. there will be crowding this planet over 6 billion human souls!

Just how many of these burgeoning billions have we evangelicals reached for Jesus Christ? Missiologist Ralph Winter's chart, "Unreached Peoples of the World 1985," shows not quite 6 percent of the world's population as being true Christian.[1] This leaves around 94 percent of the world's peoples unconverted in the true sense.

While more people in the world are being reached with the gospel, and more of them turning to Christ than ever before in the history of the church, the number of spiritually starving people is appalling. Like Jesus' disciples, too many of us Christians today view our task of feeding so many as hopeless. As the disciples reasoned then, too many of us likewise reason that the only feasible way out is to send the masses away empty. Yet, if we do send the many away without so much as once confronting them with Jesus the Bread of life, how are we going to face our Lord whose challenge to us does not change? "They do not need to go away," Jesus still insists. "You give them something to eat" (Matt. 14:16, NIV).

"Ah, but, Lord, the population explosion is not the only obstacle that bars our way. There are other dread obstacles besides. Worst of all other obstacles, there is heavy enmity to the gospel barring our way!" Nonetheless, my brethren,

In Spite of the Ever-Mounting Hostility, Still Jesus Challenges Us: "You Feed Them!"

There in the desert the disciples of Jesus felt the hostility of their environment. The very destitution of the place must have moved in on them from every quarter. Likely, unshakable human foes were present too. If so, their opposition must have been direct, deliberate, and intended to enervate. In Athens there were the intellectuals who sought to belittle both Paul and his gospel. When Paul reached the conclusion of his Mars' Hill sermon, it was likely their adverse influence turned the bulk of the people away from deciding for Jesus.

Surely ours is a hostile world today. Surely our world is a desert place, a lonely place, a hungry place. As it was with Jesus' disciples, so it is with us today: dire adversaries threaten in the shadows of advancing night. Not only are billions held hostage behind high and unscalable walls, but formidable giants of opposition guard our access to them. Deadly ideologies entangle their reasoning. Fanatical atheistic systems asphyxiate their hopes. Powerful governments like mammoth octopuses, with laws like merciless tentacles, prevent the free exercise of their basic human rights. Wicked men maintain vast sway over the captives. Most sinister of all, demonic forces of the spiritual underworld hold them in deception. These giant enemies bar our way to those held hostage by sin. Not only so, but now Christian leaders expect worsening decades ahead.

Most of the spies Moses sent forth to reconnoiter the Promised Land saw no hope of scaling the high walls surrounding the territory—how much more might the exceedingly high walls surrounding the unsaved seem to us impassable! Like the spies reporting to Moses and like the disciples in the presence of Jesus, we find ourselves complaining: "Here we are in a wilderness, Lord. Ours is a destitute situation. As You can see, we are surrounded by an environment that sternly brooks our advance into the areas of our world that are closed off to Your gospel. It's preposterous to imagine that we can cut through all of this opposition. We simply will have to send the multitudes into eternity to starve forever without You! Please understand, Jesus, we have no alternative."

But what is our Lord's answer? His answer is unchanging: "That isn't necessary—you feed them!" (Matt. 14:16, TLB).

The breath quite taken out of us by Jesus' invariable challenge that will not go away, we try again: "But, Lord, what you command us to do is strictly beyond our human capacity!" Nonetheless,

In Spite of Our Ever-disarming Inability, Jesus Still Challenges Us: "You Feed Them!"

Like the disciples, we hear ourselves objecting: "Why, in the presence of these many, we are so few!" Like Moses' disgruntled spies, we hear ourselves bemoaning our plight: "Why, in the sight of our enemies we are as grasshoppers!" (See Num. 13:33.) We so magnify our weaknesses: "How limited is our force to move against our enemies' closed ranks!"

And our human resources, how inadequate they are to feed the mushrooming multitudes! We have so little with which to perform what you charge us to do, Lord . . . Why, like the disciples, we have here, as it were, but five small loaves and two tiny fish. Even if we could get through the enemy surrounding them, how absurd to suppose that we could feed so many with so little!

And our little ones, our precious sons and daughters, Lord! What will keep them from falling prey to the forbidding enemies in control of the countries you challenge us to pray an opening into, and them to enter? (See Num. 14:3.)

Impossible challenge? Never! Never does our Lord challenge His own to an undertaking in which He will not be with us, in which He will not enable us to accomplish His task. Why, the very fact that Jesus commands us should be all we need to encourage us and to assure us of success. The fact that Jesus was with them was all the disciples needed. All that Paul needed to urge him forward was to be aware that his Commander and Leader was with him in the undertaking. Paul was by no means alone, and he knew it. What more do we Christians need than to realize that our Lord has promised to be with us always, even unto the very end? Did Jesus not keep good His promise to His first apostles (see Mark 16:20)? Has He not kept good His promise to all of His apostles since then?

What is it, then, that we need to do? Is it not, first of all, that, as Jesus' disciples did, we should present ourselves before our Lord? Is it not that, as Paul did, we should submit ourselves, body and soul, to our Lord's disposal? Is it not that, as Jesus' disciples brought the little boy to Jesus, we should bring our children to Jesus, trusting them into His hands as the safest and best of all possible places for them? Is it not, then, that, as the disciples and the little boy placed what little they had in their hands into Jesus' hands, that we and our children should place what little we have into Jesus' hands?

Then, if we do bring ourselves, our fortunes, our lives, our youth, our sacred all to Jesus, is it too much to expect that He is just as able today to perform a miracle before our very eyes? In truth, He is performing miracles before the very eyes of His servants on the mission fields of the world every day. Then, is it too much to expect that He, who once fed some 20,000 to 30,000 men, women, and children with five small loaves and two little fish, is well able to use us, our youth, and our seeming little worth to feed all of our world's hungry masses with His Bread of life?

He who once parted the formidable Red Sea, and later the forbidding Jordan, can He not provide us an entrance into as-yet-unentered countries? He who once brought down the high walls of Jericho, can He not bring down the higher walls barring our access to to the lost? Though the masses indeed are swelling in size with every passing day, though worldly opposition indeed is daily worsening, and likely to worsen far more, do we Christians not serve the same God whom Moses served; whom Joshua served; whom the disciples served; whom Paul served?

Gladly do I join ranks with the Christians who dare, as Carey once did, both to expect and to attempt great things under God in the decades ahead.

Now the Southern Baptist Foreign Mission Board tells us:

> The global challenge for the years remaining in this century is almost beyond comprehension. It underscores the priorities of God's Kingdom, as God's people do missions in the midst of political tensions, natural disasters and economic uncertainties. At the same time Charles Bryan,

the board's senior vice president for overseas operations, cites the extent of work in 106 countries as cause for rejoicing, with the reminder that we have not come to this point by happenstance.

"God opens doors," Bryan says, "but we must be ready to commit resources to enter those doors."[2]

Lift up your eyes, and look on the fields (John 4:35). His spirit was stirred to its depths to see the city (Acts 17:16, Williams).

13
Today's One Emergency

Our worst problem today is not that Christians view the task of world evangelization as overwhelming. Rather, our worst problem is that the overwhelming majority of Christians have little vision or no vision at all. If ever they have actually lifted up their spiritual eyes and looked upon the harvest fields of the world, they have straightway forgotten what they saw.

To those of His day, as well as to those of our day who are wonder when the lost world will be ripe for harvest, Jesus declares: "Say not ye, There are yet four months, and then cometh harvest? behold, I say unto you, Lift up your eyes, and look on the fields; for they are white already to harvest." Jesus calls us to see the vision of a lost world that is not going to become ripe for evangelization. It is a lost world long overripe and rotting for the lack of evangelization.

Too many of us Christians today lack a vision of

The Overripe Soul Harvest Emergency

that confronts us on every hand and to the ends of earth.

If Paul had never experienced his heavenly vision in which he saw both the risen Christ and a perishing fellow humanity, and in which he heard his Lord sending him far away unto the lost Gentiles, he never would have found himself in Athens as a missionary to begin with. (See Acts 26:14-19.) Then, once in Athens, Paul never would have borne such witness as he did to Jesus and His saving grace if he had not first had "his spirit . . . stirred to its depths to see the city completely steeped in idolatry" (Williams). Here, as in all other cities, provinces, and countries throughout his missionary itinerary, Paul ever kept his eyes upon the heavenly vision, he was never disobedient to that vision.

All about him, Paul saw the city of Athens as a field already overripe unto harvest. Likewise he recognized the limited time he had in which to harvest. Realizing that any day his Lord might call him on to other fields, he realized he must make every day count to the utmost. Therefore, every day found Paul early and late at either the synagogue or the marketplace testifying of his Savior. Once he began his discussions with the citizenry, Paul discovered how ready many were to hear more. He struck while the iron was hot.

If we Christians keep before us the heavenly vision, we are aware that the same situation prevails in our modern world. All over the globe, souls are hungry, eager, and waiting for the gospel. Long centuries of groping in heavy heathen darkness for the one Savior has prepared many hearts; desires are ripe now; consciences are awake now; expectations are aroused now; hopes are high now. The present condition of governments, the development of cultures, and the thinking of the masses constitute a situation that is desperate. As never before in history, there is an international need that we Christians must awaken to see. We must have the heavenly vision to see our Lord Jesus weeping over a world that is not only lost but rotting for lack of enough harvesters.

Doors are open now, and more doors are opening all

around our earth that are soon going to slam shut in our faces unless we enter overripe fields through them at once. Doors of entire countries, doors of entire races, doors of entire continents, are even now either open or, as many concerned Christian leaders believe, are on the verge of opening. On the verge of opening are doors long kept shut, and even doors never yet opened in all of history.

Doors are open in Central and South America. Doors are open in much of Africa where the number of Christians is growing five times faster than the population. A number of Asian countries are experiencing spiritual awakening, as South Korea, Indonesia, the Philipines, and Mainland China, even though some of these are closed and others partially closed or restricted to missionaries. In Africa and Asia alone, a thousand new churches are born every week. Many believe that an awakening is beginning in Russia, as already there is awakening in Rumania, where within months church congregations are doubling and tripling in size. Now missiologists predict that doors will soon open significantly in the Muslim world.

You may well be asking, "When will God open the securely bolted doors behind which billions are now held hostage?" I believe that God will open those doors when more of us Christians enter the multiple doors He is holding open for us already. But I feel that not until more of us take advantage of the presently wide-open doors of opportunity will God open those securely bolted doors.

We must act now and act quickly. As Paul was, so we must be, ready to strike while the iron is hot. It was Jesus who said, "I must work the works of him that sent me, while it is day" (John 9:4). We too must work while it is day.

Yet, not only do too many of us Christians lack the vision

of the overripe soul harvest emergency, but even more tragically, too many of us Christians today lack a vision of

The Imminent Judgment Harvest Emergency

now casting its heavy shadow across our sin-sick world.

The Bible speaks of not one great harvest but two. The first, the soul harvest, is one etched in glory. The second and final, the nearing-judgment harvest, is one etched in doom. One is a bright harvest; the other is a dark harvest. The bright harvest now upon is overshadowed by the dark harvest that any day will be upon us. Speaking of the judgment harvest in Matthew 13:39, Jesus tells us, "The harvest is the end of the world."

The judgment harvest is the day of final judgment for all of the lost world. Will it include those who have never heard the gospel? Definitely. In Revelation 20:12-15, we read that all peoples of all nations will be summoned before the great white throne on which sits the Almighty Judge of all the earth. John wrote, "And I saw the dead, small and great, stand before God." No person whose name does not appear written in the Lamb's book of life will be spared. Every soul whose name is not found there will be cast into the lake of fire. Jesus stated, "In the time of harvest I will say to the reapers, Gather ye together first the tares, and bind them in bundles to burn them: but gather the wheat into my barn" (Matt. 13:30).

If, then, the soul harvest is the harvest of uniting all believing people with the one God, certainly the judgment harvest is the harvest of separating all unbelieving people from the one God for all eternity!

Now if the soul harvest of the world is ripe and more than ripe, isn't the judgment harvest of the world ripe and more than ripe as well? Revelation 14:15 asserts, "The harvest of the world is ripe." For every lost human being the day of final judgment is near at hand. Some one of you may be wondering, *But if the judgment day is yet future, how could it be near for the lost in Paul's day?* Well, it was near then because Paul admonished his world as much as ours, "God . . . now commandeth all men everywhere to repent," and get ready for the judgment (Acts 17:30).

For all of those in Paul's day, and for all of those in all ages before and since who have gone out of this earthly life without repentance toward God and faith toward our Lord Jesus Christ, there is no more chance to repent and believe. Even should the great white throne judgment be a thousand years yet in the future—which I seriously doubt—for all of the unsaved dead it is very near. It is staring them in the face. "It is appointed unto men once to die, but after this the judgment" (Heb. 9:27).

The judgment likewise is near for the lost who are living in our day. It is near for them because, in comparison to eternity, life is short. It is near for them because for every human, death is certain. It is near for them because for every human the hour of death is uncertain. It is near for them because all over this earth, souls without Jesus are dying every second. Authorities estimate that an average of 6,000 persons slip out into eternity every hour. That's an average of 144,000 every day, and we know that the majority die unprepared. Now if over half the world be ignorant of Scripture, then well over half who die unprepared die totally unaware of the scriptural warning as to both the inevitability and the nearness of the judgment. Yet, just as certain, and just as near as is the day of judgment for earth's knowledgeable, just so certain and just so near is the day of judgment for earth's ignorant.

If Paul counted it his solemn responsibility before God to warn his world that "[God] hath appointed a day, in which he will judge the world in righteousness by that man whom he hath ordained" (Acts 17:31), shouldn't

Christians today count it our solemn responsibility before
God to warn our world? Shouldn't we warn our world—
including those ignorant of the gospel—that the harvest
of the world is ripe? Shouldn't we warn our world that
unless lost people repent at once, any day for them the
harvest will be past, the summer will be ended, and they
will not be saved? (See Jer. 8:20.) Jesus said, "I must work
the works of him that sent me, while it is day: the night
cometh"? We too must work while it is day because the
night is coming.

Yet, not only do too many Christians today lack the
vision of the overripe soul harvest, as well as that of the
imminent judgment harvest, but still more disastrous for
our lost world, too many of us lack a vision of

The All-Out Sacrifice Needed to Meet
Today's One Emergency

How well I remember our emergency wheat harvests
in which we labored when I was a boy growing up on my
father's farm. As wheat farmers know, when the wheat
turns golden and the heads bend low on the stalks, the
grain must be harvested within a day or two. They know
that it is now or never. Everything else must be laid aside.
They know that if, by any chance, a rain should hit the
standing grain, it means disaster. I remember some harvests on my father's farm when we really had to work in
a hurry. We would wake up in the morning to see a black,
threatening cloud hovering low over the dead-ripe
wheat. Neighbors would come pouring in to help us. Back
then one didn't have to worry about getting help at such
a time.

Right away we would help Dad roll out the old-time
binder from the tool shed and help him hitch our three
mules to it. I can see Dad now, seated high upon the
binder and leaning forth over the mules as with his check-
reins he urged them forward briskly around the field of

standing grain. I can still hear Dad call out sharply to the mules; I can still see the mules stepping out almost into a run; I can still view the sweat staining their backs and the harness.

I can still feel the hot sun burning down upon my head and the salty sweat trickling down between my shoulder blades as we workhands shocked that wheat on the run.

Oh, those were great days, but upon us Christians now are far greater, far more urgent days! We concerned Christians are now in an all-out race against time, against rapidly closing doors, against false teachers and their teachings, against all the desperate and multiple tactics of Satan.

A worldwide soul harvest is imperiled now. The judgment cloud is black and bending low. It is a field for which far-from-enough laborers are volunteering. It is a field for which far-from-enough capital is being donated to finance the colossal emergency harvest need. Above all, the emergency harvest need of the world field has far-from-enough prayer warriors.

"Tell me now," you may well be asking, "just exactly how much does our lost world need, anyway?" Let us face the need of our lost world, major need by major need.

First, how many laborers are needed? Exactly how many missionaries? Each succeeding vital conference on the unreached of the world brings to the fore both the urgency and the staggering dimensions of the task. Both evangelicals as a whole and Southern Baptist evangelicals in particular are growing more and more concerned. During the historic Consultation on World Evangelization in Pattaya, Thailand, in 1980 it was reported that the awesome proportions of the task produced such a sense of urgency that a call was sounded forth for 200,000 high-quality, well-trained North American evangelical missionaries by the year AD 2000 to deal with the emergency.

Four years earlier Southern Baptists at the launching of Bold Mission Thrust in Norfolk, Virginia, had responded to the overwhelming world need by an urgent call for 5,000 home missionaries and 5,000 foreign missionaries by the year AD 2000.

Since these respective calls, both evangelicals generally and Southern Baptist evangelicals specifically have been taking long strides toward reaching our goals. Ralph Winter's Chart for 1985 lists North American Protestant missionaries as now being 67,980 in number.[1] I am not sure whether all of these are considered evangelical Protestants. At any rate, the number is growing fast since the number of North American evangelical Protestant missionaries in 1980 was said to be some 37,000. The record 18,100 participants who attended the Inter-Varsity Christian Fellowship in Urbana, Illinois, in late 1984 was declared to have revealed a decidedly higher-than-ever interest in world missions on the part of United States college and university students. More than 85 percent of those participating indicated on their registration cards their response to long-term missionary service as either "definite," "probable," or "unsure, but open."[2]

More and more interest is being manifested by Southern Baptist college and seminary students with more than ever volunteering for home and foreign missionary service. Overall, Southern Baptist volunteers for long- and short-term service overseas was up from 1,200 in 1976 to 6,245 in 1986. Career missionaries of our Foreign Mission Board were up from 2,667 in 1976 to 3,597 by the end of 1985. Both home and foreign missionaries of the Southern Baptist Convention are fast approaching 4,000 home and 4,000 foreign.

Third World missionaries likewise are proliferating rapidly. Whereas it was stated that there were only 3,000 Third World missionaries at the convening of the International Congress on World Evangelization in Lausanne, Switzerland, in 1974, Ralph Winter brought to notice at Urbana 1984 that the Third World has already at work more than 20,000 missionaries, with some 300 mission societies operating from bases in the Third World. Winter predicted that the Third World will dominate "the era ahead of us" as to missionary outreach.[3]

Yet even with this sharp upsurge in missionary volunteers, as Winston Crawley pointed out, "It probably is still true that more than half of all Protestant and Evangelical preachers in the world are ministering in the United States. It is certain that more than 95 percent of Southern Baptist preachers remain in the United States to minister among 5 percent of the world's people."[4] Are we Southern Baptist preachers willing to let this imbalance continue? Are we willing to leave the major portion of reaching the world's unreached billions to other evangelicals and largely to Third World evangelicals?

One fact is sure. God is going to get the job done. Ralph Winter, while affirming that an effective church could be formed in each of the world's unreached peoples groups within the next few decades, also declared that "Never in history has completing the task [of world evangelization] been so feasible. This job is within our grasp."[5] Nearly 900 of the delegates at Urbana '84 indicated on their registration cards that they chose as their long-term vocational preference to minister to "unreached peoples," groups not yet exposed to the gospel.[6] And God is fast finding volunteers among Third World missionaries. So the question is not whether God will find volunteers to complete His job of reaching the unreached. Rather, the two fold question is: (1) How many of earth's unreached masses are we evangelicals going to let slip out into a Christless eternity before enough of us volunteer to go to them with the gospel; and (2) What share will you and I as individual believers choose to have in reaching the remainder of earth's every tribe and tongue of every nation? (See Matt. 24:14.)

Second, just how much money is needed to finance the world emergency harvest? Exactly how much will it cost to send the number of missionaries needed? Do you know how much it costs your foreign mission board to send out a single missionary, how much it costs to send out an average-sized missionary family? In this regard, Winston Crawley wrote: "There would be many possible ways of calculating and stating the cost of sending out and maintaining a missionary. We have generally approached this by taking rough averages, which would not apply specifically either to a single missionary or to an average-sized missionary family. A recent intricate calculation, including the cost of missionary housing, along with missionary support, travel to and from the field, vehicles and travel costs on the field, language study, schooling for missionary children, etc., came to an average of about $29,500 per missionary." Dr. Crawley went on to stress that this figure in no way represents the "salary" of a missionary.[7]

As you multiply this amount by the number of missionaries your denomination plans to send overseas by the year 2000, remember that the cost is constantly rising as inflation escalates. Now, as you are well aware, this amount is far from all that is needed moneywise. We must also count in many other expenses for capital and field work. There is the expense of building and maintaining churches, hospitals, and educational facilities; the expense of mass media; the expense of conducting evangelistic crusades; the expense of providing relief for victims of natural disaster and resulting famine; and the expense of the literature involved in all of this; and so forth. We have before us now an astronomical figure.

Even though in 1986 funds received by our Foreign

Mission Board were 50.2 percent of all Cooperative Program operating budget funds received by the SBC Executive Committee, up 3.31 percent over 1985; and even though the Lottie Moon Christmas Offering in 1986 (received in 1985) was up 3.81 percent over 1985 receipts, we are told by President Parks that "percentage growth of finances is not adequate to accomplish the aims of BMT [Bold Mission Thrust] or to undergird our overall objective of having our appropriate share in telling everyone in the world about Jesus Christ."[8]

Emergency measures are required to meet this staggering financial need. Dare to issue a big challenge, fellow ministers and other church, associational, and convention leaders. Dare to challenge your local church, if you are not already doing so, to begin giving at least 10 percent of your church budget through the Cooperative Program. Then dare to aim steadily and uncompromisingly toward the goal of 50 percent for the Cooperative Program and 50 percent for your local church needs. Pastors, dare to confront your people with such a challenge as: "Instead of giving King Jesus a Lottie Moon birthday gift of $10 or $20, why not give him a gift like you're planning to give your wife, husband, son, or daughter? Why not give Jesus $100, $200, $500, or $1000? Challenge likewise for Jesus' Annie Armstrong resurrection gift. Now let us dare to meet these challenges, fellow Christians. After giving our King a worthy gift on His birthday, sing: "Happy Birthday, Jesus!" And after giving Jesus a worthy resurrection gift, sing: "He Lives!"

You can lead your church to give generously. Working with other committed church leaders, I am one of the numerous ministers who have proved that God enables us to receive surprising results from small and medium-size churches for our home and foreign mission needs. Working with more complex church staffs that are dedicated to

God and His worldwide cause, plenty of other ministers have proved that God enables Christian leaders to have surprising results from big churches in our Convention. It can be done by God's help.

Dr. Oswald J. Smith, called by Dr. Billy Graham "the greatest living missionary statesman," has so led the People's Church of Toronto, Canada—which he founded and for years pastored, and where his son, Dr. Paul B. Smith, is now the pastor—that the People's Church now gives and raises annually in excess of one million dollars for world evangelization. Observe, if you will, what this outstanding Christian nonagenarian pinpoints as the problem in most of our churches today. He brings it all down to what we actually believe. "Not one pastor in a hundred believes that the supreme task of the church is world evangelization," he declared; "not one church in a thousand believes it; and not one Christian in ten thousand." Dr. Smith testified that he can determine this reality by a glance at the financial report of the average church. He is convinced that where we are distributing our money is a clear index as to where our chief concern is centered.[9]

Third, just how much prayer concern is needed? A world of concern. We Christians must be willing for Christ to lay the burden of lost humanity upon our shoulders. We must throw off our provincialism and our magnification of our local needs that exclude the rest of humanity. We must develop Christlike compassion for all of our fellow human beings. We must love all races, all remote tribes. We must have a special burden for those who have never heard. Like Oswald J. Smith, we need to raise the question, "Why should anyone hear the Gospel twice before everyone has heard it once?"[10]

The more we are concerned, the more fervently will we pray.

Thank God for the 139 or more Southern Baptist

churches in our United States that have now begun around-the-clock prayer ministries once a week. Churches with this ministry reach out to the hurting reached and unreached people all about them, as well as multitudes to the ends of the earth. Souls with their lives in a thousand knots, and often at the point of suicide, suddenly find that somebody cares, and most of all that God and His Son care. My friends, this is the answer.

This and small groups meeting weekly for one-half hour, one hour, two hours, all day, or all night means paying the price in prevailing prayer. Yet God requires such quality of prayer before He will reopen heaven's shut-up windows (2 Chron. 7:13-14), and rain down showers of blessing (Ezek. 34:26). How can we expect to reach our nation's more than 160 million unsaved people without another great awakening like those in our past history? Can we do it by our own programs, our own techniques, our own ingenuity, our own power? Preposterous! Three years of declining baptisms before 1986 prove this. Forty percent of Southern Baptist churches with no revival, no visitation program whatever, prove this. How are we going to reach and win the lost worldwide unless we first reach and win lost millions at home by a God-sent spiritual awakening that begins here and extends worldwide?

Even with "Good News America, God Loves You" Crusades indicating a reverse trend, we're still in desperate need of the old-time power. I join Robert Hamblin, Southern Baptist Home Mission Board vice-president for evangelism, who believes he sees awakening as our greatest hope for the future. I believe with him that God is up to something big, and the only way we can get in on it is by an all-out concert of Convention-wide prayer. Let us join the more than 30,000 Southern Baptist prayer partners who have attended Prayer for Spiritual Awakening (PSA) seminars and committed themselves to daily prayer for another mighty outpouring. J. Edwin Orr, considered by many the foremost authority on the subject, reminded us that history records no spiritual awakening that was not preceded by prevailing prayer. But above all, of what does God Himself remind us? Read Zechariah 4: "Not by might, nor by power, but by my spirit, saith the Lord of hosts" (v. 6*b*). We must accept the scriptural adjuration upon us to carry the message to the end of the earth. (See 1 Cor. 10:11.) Our age and our responsibility form the climax toward which all of the progressive teaching, work, and anticipation in all previous ages have long been tending. Ours is an unparalleled opportunity as well as an unparalleled responsibility. We must reach the whole world with the gospel in our generation because this is the apogee toward which all providence before us has been aiming and moving. Each of us who holds the distinction of being a Christian needs to listen closely and determine if he or she does not hear a still small voice asking, "Who knoweth whether thou art come to the kingdom for such a time as this?" (Esther 4:14).

And as we listen, can we not hear our Lord Jesus as He declares, "I must work the works of him that sent me, while it is day: the night cometh, when no man can work" (John 9:4)? If we believe that today's one emergency above all others is that of the overripe soul harvest of the world, should we not be working the works of Him who sent us, while it is day, because the night is coming, when no one can work?

So, let us beg God for the heavenly vision. Then once we catch the heavenly vision, let us always keep our eyes upon that vision. Let us never be disobedient to the heavenly vision. As we see souls everywhere perishing, as we see judgment clouds everywhere darkening, let us dedicate every fiber. Let us pray fervently and effectively. Let us pray without ceasing. Let us wet our pillows with tears. Let us open wide our billfolds. Let us not be sidetracked by self-interest, by pleasure, by controversy among ourselves. Let us make every sacrifice; let us lose no time; let us lose no commitment; Let us realize the urgency of our worldwide emergency because "Where there is no vision, the people perish" (Prov. 29:18).

Harlan Spurgeon, vice-president, Office of Human Resources of the Southern Baptist Foreign Mission Board, while reflecting, "I am impressed by the extent of human resources provided for us by God in our generation," went on to warn us, "If we do not rise to the vision, I fear the Southern Baptist Convention may become the greatest 'Dead Sea of human resources' the Christian era has ever known."[11]

She hath done what she could (Mark 14:8). Whom there-
fore ye ignorantly worship, him declare I unto you (Acts
17:23d).

14
What One Thing Can I Do
to Meet the Emergency?

"All right," you may be saying; "I will agree with you that all people everywhere without Jesus and His saving gospel are lost, even those to whom Jesus is completely unknown. I will likewise agree with you that Jesus has commanded us to evangelize every soul on earth, and that what He has commanded us to do He will certainly enable us to do. I will further agree that the harvest is great and wide and white, and the harvesttime must surely be short. But, after all, I am not a preacher or a missionary, and quite frankly I do not feel the Lord's calling to become either. So I have no clear idea what I as one individual can actually do about all those lost multitudes. Yet I will have to admit that once we acknowledge the truth that all the world without Jesus is lost, and, even more, once we acknowledge that this includes even those held hostage from hearing the gospel, then we have to face up to the reality that we ourselves have a role that God expects of us. But now it's just how to find exactly what that role is that's more than a little frustrating! Just tell me what one thing I can do."

I think that before any of us can do anything really effective toward making Christ known to those without Him, we ourselves need to become more fully acquainted with our Lord each day. I feel that the reason we are not making Him known to more lost people is that too many of us have not become fully enough acquainted with Him ourselves. Certainly, if we're saved we know Him personally, yet how intimately do we know Him? Isn't there a strong possibility that to the vast majority of Christians He remains largely unknown? In case you start to bristle at this, fellow Christian, ask yourself searchingly, "Do I have the same irresistible inner compulsion to make Him known to others that the first Christians had?"

Remember that when they testified, "For we cannot help speaking about what we have seen and heard" (Acts 4:20, NIV), the people "took knowledge of them, that they had been with Jesus" (Acts 4:13b). If we can help, doing all we can to make Him known to all people everywhere, then do we really know Him as Mary Magdalene did? As Peter and John did? As Paul knew Him?

Is there anything standing in your way toward getting to know your Lord that intimately? So you come to your Lord asking, "What one thing can I do?" You will recall that this was the very question the rich young ruler asked the Master. If there is any one thing lacking in your devotion to Jesus, Jesus knows exactly what it is. You can be sure, then, that He will test your dedication and point it out to you. You can be sure that He will reveal to you, as He did to the rich young ruler, what

One thing you lack

The one thing the rich young ruler lacked was the willingness to yield his all to Christ (see Mark 10:21, NIV). Our Lord will have our all or nothing. He commands us, "My son, give me thine heart" (Prov. 23:26). Our eye must be single, trained upon our Lord as our one God to the exclusion of all that is foreign to His will.

Contrast the devil's claim upon one with the claim of

Jesus Christ. The devil doesn't give a tidbit how much we claim to worship Christ, how much we do for Him, or what bombastic claims we make as to the sincerity of our devotions and service so long as he dominates any one area of our lives, any one part of us, any one nook of our hearts.

With our Lord Jesus, it is entirely the opposite. Our Lord declares that we are of no use to Him so long as Satan is permitted any advantage in our hearts and lives. John Ruskin said: "No possible compromise. Now, most people think if they keep all the best rooms in their hearts swept and garnished for Christ, that they may keep a little chamber in their hearts' wall for Belial on his occasional visits, or a three-legged stool for him in the heart's counting-house, or a corner for him in the heart's scullery, where he may lick the dishes. It won't do! You must cleanse the house of him, as you would of the plague, to the last spot. You must be resolved that as all you have shall be God's, so all you are shall be God's."[1]

The one thing that stood between the rich young ruler and his willingness to yield his all to Christ was his love of possessions. His possessions meant more to him than Christ. He lacked only one thing, but this one thing kept him from having Jesus, and Jesus from having him. This one thing the ruler lacked denied him his soul's salvation. You may already have Christ as your Savior. You may be saved. You may have yielded your all to Christ initially. But are you still as much His as the day you first accepted Him? Is there now some one thing you lack in your devotion to Him?

If you have discovered any one lack in your heart and life, what is it? It may not be the same thing the rich young ruler lacked. It does not have to be. Yet, whatever self-love, whatever pet habit, whatever besetting sin, it is keeping you from going deeper with your your Lord and

His will for your life. Unquestionably. What is your life's one obsession? Is it Christ and His Kingdom cause, or is it some pet obsession of your own?

However, our lack may not be a sin, as such, at all. It could be something entirely good in itself, yet something that is standing in the way of our all-out commitment. In many of our life situations, as well as in the question of our individual involvement in world missions, we become like Martha when Jesus visited in her home, anxious and troubled about many things. Our emphasis has become focused upon things and upon our doing things for Jesus too much on our own without first consulting Him. If this is the case, then along with Martha we need to submit to Jesus completely that we may learn of Him what

One Thing Is Needful

Martha was quite disgusted with her sister Mary because Mary was sitting quietly at the feet of the Master and remaining utterly intent upon Him, upon His wonderful face, upon His every word, upon His very presence that, actually, she was doing nothing else (see Luke 10:42). She was doing nothing toward helping Martha with the preparation needed for Jesus' meal with them and Lazarus. Even though Martha was heatedly insistent that He do so, Jesus did not censure Mary at all. Instead, it was Martha whom He gently rebuked.

"Martha, Martha, you are all hot and bothered. That which you are all wrapped up in is well and good, yes; but still it is secondary. The primary thing is what your sister Mary is all taken up with. This is the one thing that is needful."

Afterward, just a few days before Jesus' crucifixion, we see this same Mary engaged in a deed of love for which Jesus highly commended her. She brought an alabaster vase of very expensive perfume and with it anointed the head of Him who was ready to die as her beloved Savior. The sweet fragrance of this deed filled all the room and all the world through the ages. For this one thing all people in all ages from then to now have been mightily influenced toward a like devotion to Mary's Lord, whether they yield to this influence or not. It is not what Mary said, or even what she did alone that makes Mary one of the most effective evangelists of all time. It is what she *was* that made her do what she did. Jesus declared, "She hath done what she could" (Mark 14:8).

How many of us today have done what we could? How many of us are all taken up with the one thing that is needful? There is only one way that any of us can find out what one thing we can do for Jesus in our lives that will bring from Him the one commendation we all would like to hear, "You are doing what you can." That one way is to know Him better. The one way of getting to know Him better is to dislodge ourselves from all this selfish preoccupation and take time each day to remain quiet at Jesus' feet, acknowledging Him as our Lord, our Friend, our Commander, and our Leader.

We must cultivate an awareness of His presence. Daily we must look fully into His heart. If we take time for Him, He will take time to show us His will for us. He will then reveal to us what alabaster vase we have that we can bring to Him and with it express to Him, "This is what you mean to me," as well as express to all the world, "This is what Jesus can mean to you."

Only as day by day we learn to become caught up in the one thing that is needful can we have Jesus become so much a part of our living that we can say with Paul,

This One Thing I Do . . .

The one thing that Paul did above all else was not his witnessing (see Phil. 3:13). Yet his witnessing followed as an inevitable result of this one thing he did throughout his Christian life. The one thing Paul did was his never-ceasing submission of himself to Christ's constraining love. This love narrowed Paul's life to an ever-deepening and never-wavering channel. All that was either alien or secondary was excluded. Never considering himself to have reached his full potential for his Lord, Paul constantly sought to forget that which was past and always to go straight ahead with his hands stretched out toward his goal of fulfilling his high calling of God in Christ Jesus.

As we watch Paul throughout his Christian race, we see him ever laboring low at the feet of his Master. His eyes were ever upon the eyes of his Lord, observing His every communication, that he might know his Lord in a more intimate friendship. Paul wanted to more fully realize the depth of Jesus' suffering on his behalf, that he might experience the power of Christ's resurrection flowing throughout his own life. Such would lead unto the resurrection of more and more souls from spiritual death unto spiritual life.

Because Paul had come to know the risen Christ in his own heart and life, he could not keep back this knowledge from the ignorant Athenians. He actually could not selfishly keep it for himself alone. He had to share what he knew of the risen, reigning, redeeming Jesus with the uninformed people he met everywhere, so he shared with the people of Athens. Thus, both privately and publicly Paul acknowledged his Lord as Lord of all people. Gladly and unashamedly in his bold mission endeavor, Paul cried aloud to the Athenians and to the whole world both then and today, "Whom therefore ye ignorantly worship, him declare I unto you" (Acts 17:23).

Now I ask you: Can we Christians today truly know the risen Lord Jesus as Paul did and not come to think, to feel, to reach out, and to speak out boldly as Paul did, even as our Lord thinks, even as our Lord feels, and even as our Lord desires to reach out and to speak out through each of us to a perishing humanity? Can we truly come to know our Lord and not experience our eyes being trained, along with His eyes, upon a lost world groping in blind ignorance of Him? Can we truly become acquainted with King Jesus and not sense our heart compassion expanding progressively toward the four-dimensional outreach of His great heart? Can we truly comprehend the meaning of His saving gospel and not relate that gospel to all of the lost world? Can any one of us truly come to know the reigning Christ and still dodge His mandate that we colabor with Him and with all other true Christians everywhere in His stupendous global challenge?

Only as we come to see the lost world as our Lord Jesus sees it, and feel His heartbeat of compasson within us for that world, can we respond to His challenge to reach every remote tribe and individual now and later as Foreign Mission Board President Parks inspires us to respond:

"Equal partners. Do we really mean that? Do you? Do I?

"We are going to have to do some real soul searching if we are genuinely committed to the internationalization of missions.

"Global missions will happen only if we grasp the essence of the gospel—and it becomes an emotional, convictional reality in our own hearts.

"My prayer is that we will comprehend the extent of what God has in mind for His people.

"What about closed areas? What about people living where no Christians live—people who have never heard the gospel?

"What about the demands of the changing world? What does the essence of the gospel demand of us?

"If the Son of God really shines in a Christian's heart,

doesn't that heart become shaped like a globe? Isn't it stretched? Isn't a Christian heart a global heart?

"What did Jesus mean when He said those who were for Him were part of what He was doing?

"The world outside of Christ is the challenge toward which Jesus moved and toward which He sends us.

"What . . . just what if . . . we catch a glimpse of what God is up to—what He is pushing us to be?

"What if we view the world as God sees it?"[2]

My brother, my sister, in Christ, do you not agree that the primary reason we Christians have yet to declare to all the world with Paul, "Whom therefore ye ignorantly worship, him declare I unto you," is that we do not know and love our Lord to the point where we view the world as He sees it? The one thing too many of us lack is the one thing that Mary chose, the one thing that is needful, the one thing that Paul made his life's motto? Is it at all possible, my fellow Christian, to take time out each day and sit submissively at the feet of our Master, look long at His blessed face, and not grow more like Him?

If we could look deeply into His far-reaching eyes, we would see mirrored there those who are *LOST!*

Notes

Chapter 1

1. John R. Cheyne, *The Imperative Impulse* (Nashville: Convention Press, 1983), p. 93.

2. Carolyn Weatherford, ed., *God Has Done His Part...* (Nashville: Convention Press, 1977), p. 13.

3. The *Population Reference Bureau, Inc.* 2213 M Street NW, Washington, D. C. 20037. The estimated world population total is 4.9 billion as appears in the Population Reference Bureau's *1986 World Population Data Sheet,* published April, 1986. Used by permission.

4. Harley Schreck, Ph.D., research associate of Missions Advanced Research & Communication Center, a ministry of *World Vision International,* 919 West Huntington Drive, Monrovia, Cal. 91016 (in a personal letter to me).

5. Winston Crawley, retired vice-president for planning of the Southern Baptist Foreign Mission Board. 3806 Monument Avenue, Box 6767, Richmond, Va 23230 (in a personal letter to me).

6. Ralph D. Winter and D. Bruce Graham, chart: "Unreached Peoples of the World 1985." US Center for World Mission, 1605 East Elizabeth Street, Pasadena, California 91104. The US Center estimates that there are 17,000 major unreached people groups in the world as of 1985. MARC, World Vision, lists approximately 5,000 major unreached people groups for which they actually have information and which are in their database as of June, 1985.

7. Winter and Graham, MARC, World Vision.

8. Ibid.

9. MARC, World Vision.

10. David B. Barrett, ed., *World Christian Encyclopedia* (New York: Oxford University Press, 1982), p. 778.

11. Weatherford, p. 27.

Chapter 2

1. From the Koran.

2. Avery T. Willis, Jr., *The Biblical Basis of Missions* (Nashville: Convention Press, 1979), pp. 46,49-50.

3. From the Koran.

4. C. I. Scofield, ed., *The New Scofield Reference Bible* (New York: Oxford University Press, 1967), p. 25.

5. Charles John Ellicott, *Ellicott's Bible Commentary in One Volume*, cond. and ed., Donald N. Bowdle (Grand Rapids: Zondervan Publishing House, 1971), p. 44.

6. Morris Ashcraft, ed., *Mission Unlimited* (Nashville: The Stewardship Commission of the Southern Baptist Convention, 1976), p. 257.

7. See Edgar Young Mullins, *The Christian Religion in Its Doctrinal Expression* (Valley Forge: Judson Press, 1917), p. 324.

8. Matthew Henry, *Commentary on the Whole Bible*, New One Vol. ed., Leslie F. Church, ed. (Grand Rapids: Zondervan Publishing House, 1961), p. 1706.

9. William Owen Carver, *Missions in the Plan of the Ages* (Nashville: Broadman Press, 1951), pp. 34-35.

Chapter 3

1. Diane G. Woodcock, "Searching for Clues in Canton," *The Commission*, Mar. 1980, p. 12.

2. Robert Jamieson, A. R. Fausset, and David Brown, *Commentary Critical and Explanatory on the Whole Bible*, vol. 2 (Grand Rapids: Zondervan Publishing House, n.d.), p. 202.

3. John Calvin, *Institutes of the Christian Religion,* Ed. by John McNeill; trans. Ford Lewis Battles (Philadelphia: Westminister Press, 1960), pp. I,3,1.

4. Jamieson, Fausset, and Brown, pp. 224-225.

5. B. H. Carroll, *The Acts* ("An Interpretation of the English Bible"), ed. by J. B. Cranfill, new and complete (Nashville: Broadman Press, 1948). (Reprinted by Baker Book House with permission of Broadman Press, 1978), p. 323.

6. Ibid.

7. Matthew Henry, pp. 1757-1758.

8. Ione Lowman, *Non-Christian Religions* (Wheaton: Van Kampen Press, n.d.), p. 57.

9. B. H. Carroll, *The Book of Romans* ("An Interpretation of the English Bible"), edited by J. B. Cranfill, new and complete edition (Nashville: Broadman Press, 1948). (Reprinted by Baker Book House with permission of Broadman Press, 1978), p. 99.

10. Edward John Carnell, *An Introduction to Christian Apologetics*, fourth, Revised Edition (Grand Rapids: William B. Eerdmans Publishing Company, 1952), p. 160.

11. Ellicott, p. 896.

12. Matthew Henry, p. 1706.

13. Ibid.

Chapter 4

1. Russell Bradley Jones, *Gold from Golgotha* (Chicago: Moody Press, 1945), p. 49. Now published by: Kirkwood, Mo.: Impact Books. Copyright held by author.

2. Charles H. Spurgeon, *Spurgeon's Expository Encyclopedia*, vol. 8 (Grand Rapids: Baker Book House, reprinted 1978), pp. 102-103.

3. W. A. Criswell, *What a Savior!* (Nashville: Broadman Press, 1978), pp. 127-128.

Chapter 5

1. Joy Neal, "Reaching Sukumaland," *The Commission*, Apr. 1980, p. 15.

2. Robert O'Brien, "Learning to Cope in Tanzania," *The Commission*, June/July 1984, p. 28.
See *Thunder in the Valley* (© Copyright 1986, Broadman Press. All rights reserved.) by Doug and Evelyn Knapp. It presents an update of work in Tanzania, particularly the Kyela District, along with the results of Crusades (called "Jitihadas" in Swahili). The growth of churches is phenomenal. Agricultural Missonary Doug Knapp, himself a layperson, has baptized around 22,000 persons himself.

3. E. Johnson, *The Pulpit Commentary*, volume 18. Edited by H. D. M. Spence and Joseph S. Exell (Grand Rapids: William B. Eerdmans Publishing Company, 1975), p. 72.

Chapter 6

1. Billy Graham, *The Holy Spirit* (Waco: Word Books, 1978), p. 54.

2. Ibid.

3. Willis, Jr., p. 62.

4. Ibid., p. 69.

Chapter 7

1. Adapted from a script by Myrtes Mathias, "Conquering the Amazon," *The Commission*, Oct. 1978, pp. 5-7.
2. G. Campbell Morgan, *The Spirit of God* (New York, Chicago, Toronto: Fleming H. Revell Company, 1900), p. 164.
3. From Samuel Taylor Coleridge, "The Rhyme of the Ancient Mariner."
4. Oswald J. Smith, *The Cry of the World*, Revised Edition (London: Marshall, Morgan & Scott, 1972), pp. 33-34.
5. John Allen Moore, "William Carey: Rediscovering the Great Commission," *The Commission*, Apr. 1979, p. 20.
6. Ibid., p. 21.

Chapter 8

1. David M. Howard, general director of *World Evangelical Fellowship*, P. O. Box WEF, Wheaton, Illinois 60189 (in a personal letter to me).
2. The Southern Baptist Foreign Mission Board Annual Report: "*The World in View*, 1984"
3. Ibid.

Chapter 9

1. R. Keith Parks, "World in View: The Smoke of Ten Thousand Villages," *The Commission*, July 1980, p. 2.
2. R. Tuck, *The Pulpit Commentary*, 18 (1975), p. 85.
3. Baker James Cauthen quotation from "At the Astrodome in Houston During the Southern Baptist Convention," *The Commission*, Sept. 1979, p. 2.
4. From John Greenleaf Whittier, "Maud Muller."

Chapter 10

1. The Southern Baptist Inter-Agency Council document, *A Basic Understanding of Southern Baptist Missions Coordination*, p. 9.
2. E. Luther Copeland, *World Mission and World Survival* (Nashville: Broadman Press, 1985), pp. 139-140.
3. Ibid., pp. 141-144.
4. From Frederick L. Hosmer, "Forward Through the Ages."
5. John E. Kyle, Compiler, *The Unfinished Task* (Ventura, Calif.:

Regal Books, A Division of GL Publications, 1984. Copyright 1984 by Inter-Varsity Christian Fellowship, USA), p. 265.

6. Winston Crawley, *Global Mission: a Story to Tell* (Nashville: Broadman Press, 1985), p. 95.

7. Rudyard Kipling, "The Explorer," from *The Five Nations* (New York: Doubleday, Doran and Company).

8. Excerpts by Marilyn Laszlo taken from *Confessing Christ as Lord: The Urbana 1981 Compendium*, ed. John W. Alexander. © 1982 by Inter-Varsity Christian Fellowship of the USA and used by permission of Inter-Varsity Press, Downers Grove, IL 60515.

Chapter 11

1. From "Hidden Peoples?" *Missions Frontiers* (The Bulletin of the US Center for World Mission), Jan./Feb./Mar. 1985, p. 3.

2. See Edward R. Dayton, "To Reach the Unreached," Ralph Winter *et al.*, *Perspectives on the World Christian Movement: A Reader* (Pasadena, Calif.: William Carey Library, 1981), p. 587.

3. Edward R. Dayton and Samuel Wilson, eds., *Unreached Peoples '83* (Monrovia, Calif.: MARC [Missions Advanced Research and Communication Center], 1983), pp. 494-98,499.

4. See Ralph Winter, "Missions Today—A Look at the Future," comp. John E. Kyle, *The Unfinished Task*, pp. 73-74.

5. Dayton, *Unreached Peoples*, p. 587.

6. Winter and Graham, chart, "Unreached Peoples."

7. Dayton, *Unreached Peoples*, p. 589.

8. C. Peter Wagner, *On the Crest of the Wave: Becoming a World Christian* (Ventura, Calif.: Regal Books, A Division of GL Publications, 1983), p. 12.

9. Sam Wilson and Gordon Aeschliman, *The Hidden Half: Discovering the World of Unreached Peoples* (Monrovia, Calif.: MARC: Missions Advanced Research and Communication Center, n.d.), p. 70.

10. Ibid., p. 65.

11. See Winter and Graham, chart, "Unreached Peoples."

12. Wilson and Aeschliman, *Hidden Half*, p. 63.

Chapter 12

1. Winter and Graham, chart, "Unreached Peoples."

2. The Southern Baptist Foreign Mission Board Annual Report: "The World in View, 1983," pp. 25-26.

Chapter 13

1. Winter and Graham, chart, "Unreached Peoples."
2. Lawson Lau, "Urbana '84 Painted an Optimistic Picture of the Future of World Missions," *Christianity Today,* Feb. 1985, p. 47. Used by permission.
3. Ibid (quoting Winter).
4. Crawley, personal letter.
5. Lau, (quoting Winter), ibid.
6. Ibid.
7. Crawley, personal letter.
8. R. Keith Parks, "World in View: Planned Growth in Missions," *The Commission,* May 1985, p. 6.
9. Oswald J. Smith quotation from the cassette sermon: "The Supreme Task of the Church," The People's Church, 374 Sheppard Avenue East, Willowdale, Ontario M2N 3B6.
10. Smith, *The Cry of the World,* p. 83.
11. Harlan Spurgeon quotation in The Southern Baptist Foreign Mission Board Annual Report: "The World in View, 1984."

Chapter 14

1. John Ruskin as quoted by Charles Haddon Spurgeon, *Choice Sermon Notes* (Grand Rapids: Zondervan Publishing House, 1952), pp. 57-58.
2. R. Keith Parks, "The World Ahead," The Southern Baptist Foreign Mission Board Annual Report: *"The World in View, 1984,"* p. 30.